NAIS

Journal of the NATIVE AMERICAN *and*
INDIGENOUS STUDIES ASSOCIATION

VOLUME 11.2

Fall 2024

NAIS (ISSN 2332-1261) is published two times a year in spring and fall (Northern Hemisphere) by the University of Minnesota Press, 111 Third Avenue South, Suite 290, Minneapolis, MN 55401-2520. http://www.upress.umn.edu

Postmaster: Send address changes to *NAIS,* University of Minnesota Press, 111 Third Avenue South, Suite 290, Minneapolis, MN 55401-2520.

Information about manuscript submissions can be found at naisa.org, or inquiries can be sent to journal@naisa.org.

Books for review should be addressed to *NAIS* Journal, Centre for Indigenous Research and Community-Led Engagement, The University of Victoria, 3800 Finnerty Road, Saunders Annex 130C, Victoria, BC, V8P 5C2, Canada.

Address subscription orders, changes of address, and business correspondence (including requests for permission and advertising orders) to *NAIS,* University of Minnesota Press, 111 Third Avenue South, Suite 290, Minneapolis, MN 55401-2520.

SUBSCRIPTIONS

- **Individual subscriptions to *NAIS*** are a benefit of membership in the Native American and Indigenous Studies Association. NAISA's tiered membership ranges from $25 to $100 annually. To become a member, visit http://naisa.org/.
- For current **institutional subscriptions** and **back issue** prices, please visit: http://www.upress.umn.edu.
- **Digital subscriptions to *NAIS* for institutions** are now available online through Project MUSE at https://muse.jhu.edu.

NAIS

Journal of the NATIVE AMERICAN *and* INDIGENOUS STUDIES ASSOCIATION

CONTENTS

VOLUME 11 ● ISSUE 2

Fall 2024

Articles

Reviews

CHADWICK ALLEN

Post-Removal Mounds: Earthworks Rising in Oklahoma

Abstract

Twenty-first-century Oklahoma—where so many Southeastern, Ohio Valley, Mississippi Valley, and other mound-building and mound-stewarding peoples were forcibly removed in the nineteenth century—is witnessing a reactivation of Indigenous practices of building and stewarding large-scale, highly graphic, multiply encoded earthworks. Replicas of historical platform mounds feature prominently at the Chickasaw Cultural Center that opened in rural south-central Oklahoma in 2010 and the Choctaw Cultural Center that opened in rural southeastern Oklahoma in 2021, while a futuristic, spiraling "promontory mound" forms an integral component of the multitribal First Americans Museum that opened outside urban Oklahoma City in 2021. Constructed and curated to meet the expectations of both tribal citizens and diverse Native and non-Native tourists, how do these new earthen structures and their contextualizing environments occupy space, organize relations, and make meaning within their specific contexts of cultural celebration, Indigenous-centered education, and immersive visitor experience? And what do they tell us about the possibilities for Indigenous aesthetics and architectural design in the future?

The larger circle, outlined by the mound, represents the people who were here before us, the ancient cultures that were here in Oklahoma. The small circle represents the modern world, and the Hall of The People is the intersection of those worlds.

—JAMES PEPPER HENRY (KAW AND MUSCOGEE), QUOTED IN *FIRST AMERICAN ART MAGAZINE* (2021)

As a form of knowing, site thinking is concretely situated, more interactive than abstract, and less concerned with the semantic content of knowledge than with a concern for relationships among knowers and known. The site provides for a situation that guides what knowers do and how the known responds and can be understood.

—ANDREA KAHN AND CAROL J. BURNS, "WHY SITE MATTERS" (2021)

SUMMER SOLSTICE 2023. I am standing at a North American crossroads, in view of Oklahoma City's prairie skyline, near the junction of Interstate 35 (cars and trucks bustling north and south) and Interstate 40 (cars and trucks bustling east and west) and a calm stretch of the Canadian River known by an honorific as the Oklahoma River. Despite the June heat and the threat of a late thunderstorm, I am marking the longest day of the Northern Hemisphere's solar year with longtime friends LeAnne Howe, the award-winning Choctaw writer and intellectual, and Jim Wilson, her husband and a trained archaeologist, who have driven up from their home in Ada.[1] We join the large crowd assembled on the outdoor Festival Plaza that is central to the First Americans Museum (FAM), the state-of-the-art facility built to honor contemporary Oklahoma's thirty-nine tribal nations, opened with great fanfare in 2021. A marquee erected near the center of the plaza shades the event's lively emcee and talented drum group. Families and friends visit on lawn chairs or brightly patterned blankets; food trucks offer cold drinks and snacks; tribal royalty circulate in their regalia and sashes, smiling at everyone they meet and greeting their elders; trails of laughing children chase each other across the grass, pausing their play to inspect the demonstration tipi and brush arbor that also have been erected for the evening's festivities. Overhead, an occasional hawk circles, tracing the contours of this multiply pulsing circle on the ground. We relax into light conversation and the pleasures of the music and people-watching; it is a diverse group that has committed to this evening. More than the conviviality of the crowd, though, what I am most struck by is the way the drum's rhythm and timbre seem to hold in this space built for gathering nations—the earth and the people's collective heartbeat cradled by the circumference of the museum's massive, spiraling mound. In the words of FAM director James Pepper Henry, this large circular enclosure represents the people who were here long before us. They remain with us still, I think, in soil and in spirit.

When the evening crosses the eight o'clock hour, the emcee quiets the drum and directs attention toward the western sky. We stand to watch the setting sun slip between wisps of white cloud, fulfilling its promise to align with the ninety-foot summit of the mound. For an exquisite moment, a bright prismatic ball balances precisely upon the apex of this constructed horizon. The hushed crowd subtly shifts position to enhance the experience of alignment, raising readied cameras and smartphones high. When the moment passes, we spontaneously cheer, some of the women trilling the high-pitched *lulululu* of tribal affirmation. And as if cued, the waiting sky closes in. Although now obscured, the ball of the sun continues its descent behind the circular embankment of earth; the denser cloud mass is set ablaze from below. The emcee leads us in a prayer of gratitude for the miracle of another solar year and, when prompted, we turn as one body to acknowledge the Creator's gifts represented by the four directions: first facing east toward the mound's pathway set between the glass-and-steel Hall of The People and the stone-and-steel museum (*pause for stillness and breath*); then south toward the mound's rising embankment alive with summer grasses, small birds, and insects (*pause for stillness and breath*); then west toward the mound's dramatic alignments to the solstices (*pause for stillness and breath*); then north toward the mound's grand, emblematic opening to the arterial river (*pause for stillness and breath*). *Aho*. To conclude this celebration and giving of thanks, the emcee invites the drummers to take up their drumsticks once again, and he invites all of us gathered within the cradle of the spiraling mound—young and old, local and from afar, Native and non-Native . . . those currently embodied and those passed into soil and spirit—to join the living circle and dance.

Architectural Design as Indigenous Futurity

Descendants of mound-building and mound-stewarding peoples forcibly removed to what is now the settler state of Oklahoma are taking control of contemporary discourses on ancient mounds and other earthworks—not only through the creation of tribally-based publications and other self-representations produced in multiple media but also through the building and curation of tribally specific cultural centers and multitribal museums, including the multitribal First Americans Museum (FAM).[2] The immersive exhibits and innovative signage developed for these facilities are intended to appeal to multiple publics. As assertions of Indigenous intellectual sovereignty, both new construction and new curation actively "re-story" mounds and other earthworks against the accounts produced in previous decades by standard museology and orthodox scholarship, which typically prioritize the perspectives, desires, and needs of U.S. settler cultures, to prioritize, instead, the perspectives, desires, and needs of local tribal citizens and descendants.[3] But not exclusively. Citizens and descendants of regional tribal nations, other Indigenous Peoples from near and far, and predominantly non-Native U.S. and international tourists, are similarly acknowledged as primary audiences and welcomed as visitors. And, as suggested by my account of the solstice celebration at FAM, these efforts to recontextualize, re-present, and re-narrate ancient mounds and mound-building cultures are being conducted in tandem with active building *outside* the walls of these state-of-the-art centers and museums. That is, visual, aural, haptic, and discursive re-storying through immersive exhibits and innovative signage is being conducted in tandem with restoring the meticulous design and careful construction of large-scale, Indigenous-controlled earthen structures. These new mounds stand adjacent to—or, as at FAM, integrated with—the glass, steel, wood, and stone walls of modern, high-tech facilities.[4] Once built, these twenty-first-century earthworks are conspicuously cared for, not only physically maintained but also culturally stewarded.[5] Moreover, as demonstrated during the solstice celebration, these new mounds are actively engaged by multiple, often intersecting categories of interlocutors (diverse Native and non-Native caretakers and visitors) and through multiple, often intersecting modes of encounter (visual, physical, cultural, intellectual, emotional, spiritual).

The phrasing for my primary title, therefore, is doubly intentional. More than a temporal marker, *post-Removal* contextualizes twenty-first-century earthworks construction, use, and care by explicitly naming the violent expulsion of mound-building and mound-stewarding peoples from their ancient and historical homelands in the Southeast, the Ohio Valley, the Mississippi Valley, and other parts of what is now the U.S. settler nation-state, beginning in the 1830s, to what was then known as the Indian Territory, now known as the U.S. state of Oklahoma.[6] Forced removal is among the most egregious of the techniques of violent dispossession deployed by the United States in order to claim as part of its collective settler patrimony—and in order to incorporate as part of its collective settler imaginary—sites of archaeological, historical, and ongoing spiritual and practical importance to Indigenous Peoples. Coerced movement and militarized resettlement physically separated Indigenous Peoples from their significant pasts, impairing the ability of individuals, families, communities, and nations to maintain ongoing relations not only with their historic places, commemorative environments, and sacred sites but also with the agentive ancestral and spiritual forces with which these land-, water-, and skyscapes had been imbued for hundreds—in many cases, for thousands—of years.[7]

When activists, scholars, and community members describe the role of the arts in securing Indigenous sovereignties, they tend to focus on oral, alphabetic, syllabic, and graphic traditions as well as on a wide range of visual, textile, and plastic arts traditions, and on more recent "new" and "mixed" media traditions that help create and disseminate Indigenous knowledges and help build and sustain Indigenous communities. Typically, less attention is devoted to the role that might be played by Indigenous architectural design—the imagining, visualization, and then creation of Indigenous structures, landscapes, and other built environments—whether ancient, historical, or contemporary. But both popular and scholarly narratives are expanding in this respect, as evidenced by an increasing number of publications that spotlight contemporary achievements in Indigenous architectural design, practice, and theory.[8]

Inspired by these works, in the conclusion to *Earthworks Rising: Mound Building in Native Literature and Arts,* published in 2022, I begin an argument that I now want to extend through this essay.[9] Namely, that in what is now the U.S. state of Oklahoma, where so many Southeastern, Ohio Valley, Mississippi Valley, and other mound-building and mound-stewarding peoples were forcibly relocated in the nineteenth century, we are witnessing nothing less than a reactivation of Indigenous traditions of building and stewarding large-scale earthworks.[10] And we are witnessing, as well, a revival of Indigenous traditions of architectural diversity, complexity, and sophistication, for these new mounds are being designed and built in not one but several distinct styles or, as a scholar trained primarily in literary studies, what I want to call several distinct *genres.* As noted, since these new mounds are being constructed as integral components of public venues for Indigenous self-representation—as part of tribally specific cultural centers and multitribal museums—each is designed to appeal to the needs and desires of both Native and non-Native audiences and interlocutors.

How do these new earthen structures and their contextualizing environments occupy space, organize relations, and make meaning within their specific contexts of cultural celebration, Indigenous-centered education, and immersive visitor experience? And what do they tell us about the possibilities for Indigenous aesthetics and architectural design in the future? In the sections that follow, I begin to answer these questions by drawing from methodologies for Indigenous literary and cultural analysis (with which I am most familiar) but also from methodologies for architectural analysis, methodologies for site analysis (i.e., thinking about a specific site's material conditions), and methodologies for what some architecture scholars call "site thinking" (i.e., thinking about site as a conceptual construct) to better understand both the innovations and the continuities of the designs show-cased in Oklahoma's post-Removal mounds.[11]

Non-Native architectural historian Paul Goldberger begins his 2022 popular overview *Why Architecture Matters* by citing the general maxim that "architecture is a conversation between generations, carried out across time" (xi).[12] The statement echoes James Pepper Henry's description of the innovative design of First Americans Museum in Oklahoma City. But for the Indigenous architecture embodied at FAM and other sites, we need to expand Goldberger's maxim to explicitly acknowledge that built environments are conversations not only between human generations but also among human generations and other-than-humans, including animals and plants, rocks and soils, celestial beings, and spiritual forces. Oklahoma's post-Removal mounds can be situated within the standard classification of "historical architecture," that is, when architects choose to design new structures within the conventions and compositional logic of older or even ancient styles (think neogothic or neoclassical public buildings, or contemporary homes designed to resemble those constructed during the Victorian, Federal, or Tudor eras).[13] Goldberger states that while it is possible for architects to "simply copy what has been said before," projects in historical architecture also offer the "chance to say new things in an existing language" (193). The Indigenous mounds built in twenty-first-century Oklahoma epitomize the seizing of this chance.

The builders of these new earthworks understand the ancient principles that undergird Indigenous North American mounds: the power of layering diverse materials to create durable structures, the power of multiple simultaneous alignments to structure experience and encode knowledge.[14] But the builders also understand the contemporary contexts of their production: the dominant settler culture's disruption of Indigenous lifeways and knowledges, the dominant imaginary's relegation of Indigenous Peoples to the distant past.[15] If all architecture is a form of communication for ideas and values; if all architecture is simultaneously material form and abstract symbol; if all architecture is potentially a public presence and unifying social force; if all architecture creates orienting devices and directional spaces that guide human (and other-than-human) movement—what do these new constructions in Oklahoma "say" in the ancient language of North American earthworks, and what, in particular, do they "do" for their contemporary communities?[16]

Mounds Historical, Mounds Futuristic

In one style or genre, the tribally-specific Chickasaw Cultural Center, which opened in 2010 in a rural setting outside the town of Sulphur, Oklahoma, has constructed what the Nation calls a "replica ceremonial mound"—a large, single-terrace earthen platform.[17] Similarly, the tribally-specific Choctaw Cultural Center, which opened in 2021 in a rural setting outside the town of Durant, Oklahoma, has constructed what the Nation also calls a "replica ceremonial mound"—a massive, truncated pyramidal platform that measures four-hundred-twenty-feet long by three-hundred-feet wide at the base and that rises to a height of thirty-nine feet. The new Choctaw mound has an added distinction, however. Unlike the Chickasaw, the Choctaw have created not a generic replica but rather one that cites a specific precedent constructed in their pre-Removal Southeastern homelands: the new mound cites the ancient Nanih Waiya, located in what is now northern Mississippi.[18] In a different style or genre, the multitribal First Americans Museum, which, as noted, honors the thirty-nine tribal nations in contemporary Oklahoma and which opened in 2021 in an urban setting within view of the Oklahoma City skyline, has constructed what it calls a twenty-first-century "promontory mound"—a massive spiral of packed earth that circles a thousand-foot diameter and rises to a height of ninety feet.[19]

The juxtaposition of these distinctive styles or genres of post-Removal mounds is striking and, at first glance, appears to present a straightforward binary of primary orientations. The tribally specific "replica" mounds operate, at least in part, through processes of citation; they appear oriented primarily to the pre-Removal Southeastern past. The multitribal "promontory" mound operates—again, at least in part—through processes of innovation; it appears oriented to the post-Removal Oklahoma present and future. The Chickasaw Cultural Center, for example, situates its replica ceremonial mound within its re-creation of a Chikasha Inchokka' ("Chickasaw house"), a "historically accurate," eighteenth-century, "traditional" pre-Removal Southeastern village—that is, a life-sized historical diorama complete with similar replicas of summer and winter family houses, a large council house, a stickball court, a dance arena built around a central fire and flanked by brush arbors, and a working garden, all surrounded by a wood stockade and set beside the moving waters of Rock Creek.[20] The mound and its contextualizing environment are thus situated adjacent to but apart from the center's state-of-the-art modern buildings and high-tech facilities. Similarly, the Choctaw Cultural Center situates its replica of the Nanih Waiya within what it calls a Living Village, a large outdoor "surrounding space" located behind its state-of-the-art modern building and high-tech facilities that, in addition to the massive earthen platform, includes a dance circle, a stickball demonstration field, a garden for heirloom Choctaw crops, and examples of traditional Choctaw houses. In marked contrast, First Americans Museum, built on a restored Superfund site along an urban stretch of river that was once a grimy oilfield and a dumping ground for old tires and toxic waste, situates its massive promontory mound as a fully integrated component of its state-of-the-art modern building and high-tech facilities. The mound's rising embankment forms one of the intersecting arcs and half circles of the site's innovative architectural design, with the spiraling mound literally emerging from the ascending pathway situated between the main stone-and-steel museum building and the soaring glass-and-steel structure known as the Hall of The People (the latter modeled after the grass lodges constructed by the Wichita and Caddo peoples who lived in what is now central Oklahoma long before the United States implemented its policies of forced removal). Each of these new mounds serves important functions within its specific contexts of cultural celebration, Indigenous-centered education, and immersive visitor experience. But where the two replicas appear designed to help visitors access aspects of a specific Indigenous past, the promontory appears designed to help visitors imagine possible Indigenous futures.

Since completing *Earthworks Rising*, I have begun to question both the accuracy and the usefulness of a binary that so clearly separates the "historical" from the "futuristic." And I have begun to question, as well, whether an orientation to strictly linear, homogenous time—what some scholars designate as "universalist" clock time or, more pointedly, "colonial" or "settler" time—is an adequate basis for organizing an analysis of how large-scale, post-Removal mounds produce meaning for their multiple Native and non-Native audiences and interlocutors.[21] From what other perspectives might we more fully engage these remarkable structures as simultaneously practical, symbolic, and aesthetic entities? What other kinds of questions might we ask of them—and of ourselves in relation to their orienting presences?

Replicas—or Reactivations?

I have been visiting the Chickasaw Cultural Center since it opened in 2010, and in *Earthworks Rising* I analyze what I call the "living earthworks vocabularies" displayed in the center's indoor and outdoor signage.[22] After visiting First Americans Museum while it was still under construction in 2019, however, and then visiting several times again after its opening in 2021, both on my own and accompanied by others, I have begun to rethink my assumptions about how the replica ceremonial mound makes meaning within the larger contexts of the conspicuously dioramic outdoor "traditional village" and the conspicuously high-tech indoor exhibit facilities that comprise the center. Re-viewing the "historical" mound through the lens of the "futuristic" mound has helped me to better appreciate the complexity of the Chickasaw Cultural Center's overall design and to ask better questions about how the center orients visitors to its so-called replica and its re-created context.

In other words, I have begun to ask not only how the explicit instruction of the center's carefully worded exhibit signage works to re-story both the immediate presence of the new mound and the broader histories of mound-building and mound-stewarding peoples but also how the more *implicit* interpretive cues that are embedded within the center's carefully designed built environment similarly work to recontextualize, re-present, and re-narrate the presence of the new mound and the histories of mound-building and mound-stewarding peoples.

Unlike the tribally specific Chickasaw Cultural Center, which physically separates its replica mound from its state-of-the-art modern buildings and high-tech facilities (this is also true of the tribally specific Choctaw Cultural Center), the multitribal First Americans Museum can be understood as an explicit cyborg. As noted, the museum's spiraling promontory mound, its arced wood-stone-and-steel gallery space, and its soaring glass-and-steel Hall of The People are not simply linked but fully integrated; more precisely, these interlocked distinct components are co-constitutive. Moreover, FAM's earthen structure itself can be understood as an innovative hybrid: the mound combines ancient practices of constructing large-scale geometric enclosures—earthen outlines of mathematically encoded circles, squares, and octagons, such as the massive earthen enclosure known as the Great Circle in what is now central Ohio—with ancient practices of constructing large platforms, such as the terraced and truncated earthen pyramids integrated into the rise of the Crawfish River Valley at the site known as Aztalan in what is now southern Wisconsin. Similar to a geometric enclosure, FAM's new mound has been designed to demarcate ceremonial space, what the museum designates as the Festival Plaza; and similar to a platform, FAM's new mound has been designed not only for visual but also for direct physical engagement. In contrast to the Chickasaw and Choctaw cultural centers, where signage, guardrails, fences, and staff explicitly prohibit visitors from climbing or walking on the newly constructed mounds, First Americans Museum invites visitors to traverse a paved pathway along its mound's curving ascent up to the ninety-foot promontory, where they can enjoy expansive views of the surrounding environment, including the Oklahoma City skyline to the northwest, the FAM complex to the immediate southeast, and other examples of economic, civic, and cultural constructions along the river.[23] Also similar to ancient platform sites, FAM has been designed to combine a large mound with other built structures, such as the log-and-thatch civic and ceremonial buildings that were constructed on top of the large earthen platforms at the thousand-year-old mound city sites known as Cahokia in what is now southern Illinois and Moundville in what is now central Alabama.[24]

In addition, similar to many if not most ancient earthworks sites, First Americans Museum is oriented not only to water but also to major trails and roadways.[25] As noted, FAM is sited at the major transportation interchange where Interstate 35, a primary, continental artery running north and south between Texas and Minnesota, crosses Interstate 40, a primary, continental artery running east and west between California and North Carolina.[26] Finally, also similar to many ancient earthworks sites, FAM is oriented to the cardinal directions and to major solar phenomena. The facility's front doors open east to sunrise, and additional features of both the stone, wood, glass, and steel building and the earthen mound align to the equinoxes and solstices so that the site as a whole functions as a massive cosmological clock attuned to both daily and seasonal time. As described in my opening narration, at sunset on the longest day of the Northern Hemisphere's solar year, about June 21, the ball of the evening sun sets precisely behind the high point of the promontory's concluding ledge (see figure 1). At sunset on the shortest day of the Northern Hemisphere's solar year, about December 21, beams of evening's last light shoot through a large tunnel constructed precisely at the right location along the arc of the rising embankment.

FIGURE I. View of the summer solstice sunset alignment with the promontory mound at First Americans Museum. Photograph by Chadwick Allen.

When FAM opened to the public in September 2021, its small Community Gallery featured a temporary exhibit titled *Of the Earth: Creating First Americans Museum,* which explained the site's overall design and construction history through detailed signage, multiple images, and an evocative 3D scale model. The signage described the new building and its accompanying earthwork as a "21st century mound" that "references" tribal histories and key relationships:

> Our new home embodies our values. Conceived as a 21st century mound, our addition to the Oklahoma City skyline proclaims the vibrancy of our cultures. Once an oilfield, our campus is green and lush. The design of our building and mound references our tribal histories and relationship to the earth, sky and cosmos.

Two enlarged photographs emphasized the new mound's two primary solar alignments (and provided opportunities for visitors to take selfies with the solstices). The exhibit's model, however—which was circular in shape, neutral in color, and about the size of a large dining room table—did more than offer a static representation of the new building and mound frozen at a particular moment in time. Rather, unlike the still images of the solstices, the model offered a *dynamic* representation of how the site's alignments change across time, understood at multiple scales—or, perhaps more precisely, understood through multiple periodicities. A projector mounted in the ceiling cast still and moving images onto the broad, flat rim surrounding the circumference of the model; on a regular loop, color projections marked the site's directional orientations, listed the thirty-nine tribal nations currently residing in Oklahoma, and displayed brief quotations from Indigenous elders and intellectuals. The projector cast still and moving images, as well, onto the 3D surface of the model's interior, which depicted the contours of the arcs and circles of the building and mound in a monochromatic off-white. Here, the sequence of projections commemorated the site's ground blessing ceremony and chronicled various stages of the facility's complex construction. The bright, shifting images at play upon the monochromatic 3D model brought the drama of the site's recent history to vibrant life. But the model's most profound theatricality occurred when the projected images demonstrated how the site's solar alignments progress both across an individual day and across the annual seasons (see figure 2). With the cardinal directions marked on the model's flat rim like the face of a compass, the bright ball of the sun was made to travel from east to west in a banding arc, first dramatically crossing the half-circle of the building with its entry oriented to shifting sunrise (from equinox to equinox) and then dramatically crossing the spiraling mound with its tunnel and promontory oriented to shifting sunset (from solstice to solstice).

FIGURE 2. The dynamic scale model of First Americans Museum demonstrates the daily and seasonal movements of the sun. Photograph by Chadwick Allen.

Experiencing these dynamics of First Americans Museum's scale model sent me back to the Chickasaw Cultural Center to rethink how its mound functions within the Chikasha Inchokka', the life-sized model of an eighteenth-century Southeastern village, as well as within the center as a whole. A map of the 184-acre campus demonstrates how the "traditional" village relates to other features of the site.[27] Visitors are oriented to encounter the village first from the constructed vista of the three-story Aba' Aanowa' ("a place for walking above") Sky Bridge located adjacent to the main exhibit buildings. Here, visitors can survey the expansive scene of the village, including its mound, from an ideal height and distance, what is conventionally understood as a position of visual mastery (see figure 3). The potential implications of this idealized perspective or bird's-eye view—what is sometimes described more provocatively as a God's-eye view—have been discussed extensively within studies of colonial discourses, where to *survey* from a dominant position is often understood as to *surveil* and therefore to control.[28] Importantly, however, having surveyed (or surveilled) the scene from this unobstructed perspective forty feet above the replica, visitors can descend *into* the village, by means of either an efficient but steep set of stairs or a meandering but more accessible pathway, where they experience a significant shift in both visual perspective and embodied experience. On the ground, sightlines are necessarily partial, and views are often obstructed. One observes the mound through the shifting movements of a stomp dance performed around the central fire of the outdoor arena, for example, or from under the shade of a brush arbor. Or one moves to the far side of the village, turns around, and observes the mound from behind. But this angle is "behind" the mound only from the colonial perspective of the Sky Bridge. Hundreds or thousands of years ago, a mound village or mound city would have been oriented to a central waterway; the dynamic current of Rock Creek, rather than a static bridge to the sky, would have anchored a typical visitor's perspective.

Situated within the Chikasha Inchokka', visitors can observe not only the Sky Bridge's juxtaposition with the replicas of "traditional" log-and-thatch structures, such as the large council house, but also the full height of the steel structure and the complexity of its contemporary design and engineering (see figure 4). In other words, whereas the experience of viewing the village from the Sky Bridge conceals the modern technology that enables a visual perspective associated with colonial mastery, making that dominating perspective appear natural, the experience of viewing the Sky Bridge

FIGURE 3. View from the Sky Bridge at the Chickasaw Cultural Center during a stomp dance performed before the replica ceremonial mound at the Chikasha Inchokka', the center's Southeastern-style village. Photograph by Chadwick Allen.

FIGURE 4. View of the Sky Bridge from within the Chickasaw Cultural Center's Chikasha Inchokka'. Photograph by Chadwick Allen.

from within the village exposes the role of this technology in framing visitors' experience. The view from within the re-created eighteenth-century village reveals the limited and highly constructed nature of dominant perspectives on Indigenous cultures, perhaps especially the limited and highly constructed nature of dominant perspectives on Indigenous histories that span hundreds or thousands of years. In this way, the Chickasaw Cultural Center exposes rather than conceals its active participation in shaping how visitors construct their understandings of the replica ceremonial mound.

The repeated labeling of the mound as a "replica" on official maps and posted signage makes an emphatic statement that the earthen structure to which visitors have visual and embodied access is *not* a ghost of the past, is *not* a revenant returned from the dead, is *not* a witness to ancient Indigenous histories. That is, the mound is *not* authentic in the ways that dominant, non-Native U.S. culture tends to construct—and often attempts to manage or control—Indigenous authenticity. No, as a *replica,* the earthen structure to which visitors have visual and embodied access is an explicitly *new* creation located in the contemporary moment. It is both recently constructed and meant to endure over time. Although the replica is set within the framework of "historical reenactment," within what amounts to a living diorama of a "traditional" Southeastern village, its life exists not in the Chickasaw Nation's Southeastern past but in its Oklahoma present—and in its future still to come. Unlike a *relic,* the replica's authenticity lies not in its asserted material continuity with the past but in its active response to its makers' and caretakers' contemporary needs and desires. These needs and desires manifest in decisions to present aspects of the Chickasaw past to outside visitors in specific and highly proscribed ways. They manifest as well in the active exposure of the coloniality of dominant forms of U.S. settler knowledge about Indigenous Peoples.[29]

We might ask, then, whether the replica's function is primarily *aesthetic* (concerned with a philosophy of representation) rather than primarily *historical* (concerned with past events) or *antiquarian* (concerned with antiquities, that is, aspects of the ancient past). My sense is that the answer is yes, the replica's function is primarily aesthetic, in that it presents an idealized form of a Southeastern platform, covered in a species of grass that requires minimal maintenance, surrounded by a low guardrail to prevent damage from visitors, and marked by explanatory signage that frames visitors' understandings of Chickasaw history and living culture.[30] The replica does not bear witness to the history of the actual ground upon which it stands, nor of the soil from which it was literally formed in rural south-central Oklahoma. Whether or not all visitors understand these details, of course, is another question, but there is little ambiguity in so prominently labeling the mound a replica.

Here I would draw attention to the low guardrail as well as to the posted signage: the replica is meant to be viewed both at a distance and up close, but it is not meant for direct physical encounter (see figure 5). Although newly constructed, unlike the mound at First Americans Museum, the mound at the Chickasaw Cultural Center was not designed to be walked upon or otherwise traversed by visitors (this is also true of the replica ceremonial mound at the Choctaw Cultural Center, which is surrounded by substantial mesh fencing). In one sense, the platform is all form and no function. But this observation rests on a narrow understanding of *function.* A replica mound built by a sovereign Indigenous nation forcibly removed from its historical homelands is still an Indigenous mound. And perhaps the mound's designation as "ceremonial" requires additional scrutiny. To my knowledge, no ceremonies or rituals of any kind are performed on the mound's surface. Stomp dances are performed around the central fire adjacent to the mound and at other indoor and outdoor performance spaces located across the center's campus. A marked path and signage positioned at multiple locations invite visitors to circumambulate the platform mound—which could constitute a kind of ritual—but the guardrail makes clear that visitors are not to stray from the designated route.

FIGURE 5. Low guardrail and signage posted near the replica ceremonial mound at the Chickasaw Cultural Center's Chikasha Inchokka'. Photograph by Chadwick Allen.

Indeed, the Chickasaw Cultural Center is exceptionally deliberate in guiding its mostly non-local, non-Native visitors in how they should view and in how they should encounter the new mound. The repeated use of the adjectives *replica* and *ceremonial* contributes to this deliberate guidance: together, the stacked adjectives emphasize not what the mound *is,* but rather what the mound emphatically *is not.* The mound is neither "authentic" nor "functional" within the dominant settler culture's typical understandings of these concepts. Which is to say, similar to FAM's promontory mound, the Chickasaw Cultural Center's ceremonial mound is emphatically *not* a burial site.[31] Designating the mound as both a replica and ceremonial interrupts pervasive settler speculation that all mounds are sites of interment. Dominant, non-Native U.S. culture tends to assume that all mounds were (and therefore are) used for burial, that all mounds were (and therefore are) full of Indigenous human remains and other potentially valuable archaeological "treasure."[32] Ironically, within the context of the Chickasaw Cultural Center, the adjective *ceremonial* does not indicate a location or structure intended for the performance of civic or sacred ritual, but rather asserts the mundane and even profane nature of the site in order to deflect a certain kind of potentially harmful settler attention.

Although the Chickasaw Cultural Center's twenty-first-century mound is not as obviously dynamic—in the sense that it is not as obviously theatrical—as First Americans Museum's twenty-first-century mound with its dramatic solar alignments, it too represents a reactivation of Indigenous technologies, practices, and ideas. Part of the center's tribally specific maneuver is to reactivate Indigenous sovereignty over the visual display of and physical encounter with Chickasaw history, including Chikasha history from the pre-Removal deep past.

Ascending the Mound

After conducting a re-analysis of the Chickasaw Cultural Center and its "historical" mound, I soon found myself in a position to reanalyze, as well, the First Americans Museum and its "futuristic" mound. As noted, I first visited FAM in 2019 when it was still under construction, an event I describe in the conclusion to *Earthworks Rising,* and then visited again in 2021, when the museum first opened to the public.[33] Not all components of the facility, however, had been completed, including the pathway that allows visitors to ascend the mound. In 2021, the pathway was still unpaved, the safety rail still uninstalled, and the explanatory signage still unposted. I was able to visit FAM again in the spring and summer of 2023 and was able to engage these aspects of the museum's immersive, embodied experience for the first time.[34]

When I visited FAM in March 2023, *Of the Earth: The Making of First Americans Museum* had been removed from the Community Gallery and replaced with a different exhibit, but the Mound Path was now complete. Where the temporary exhibit's 3D scale model had invited visitors to view the interlocking building and mound and their immediate environment from an idealized aerial perspective (as though visitors were positioned at a great height above the museum complex) and to experience the site's directional orientations and multiple temporalities through the use of projected still and moving images, the Mound Path invites visitors into an embodied and multisensory experience of moving along the mound's paved pathway, which circles the thousand-foot diameter of the Festival Plaza, slowly rising to the ninety-foot summit. Unlike viewing the scale model from within the gallery, which offered visitors a simulated, time-elapsed experience of the daily and seasonal movements of the sun under ideal viewing conditions, physically moving along the Mound Path necessarily creates different experiences depending on the time of day, time of year, and specific weather conditions visitors encounter. In contrast to my visit in 2019, for instance, which occurred on a rainy, overcast afternoon in late October, my first visit in 2023 occurred a few days past the vernal equinox, on a bright afternoon in late March, when the sun was high in a mostly clear sky with only a few clouds.

Visitors' experience of ascending the Mound Path is framed by contextualizing signage located inside the glass-and-steel Hall of The People, which describes the new structure as the work of "21st Century Mound Builders" (see figure 6). Similar to the *Of the Earth* temporary exhibit, the new signage includes still images of the sunset alignments to the summer and winter solstices, with captioning that asserts the ongoing significance of marking these solar phenomena and celestial events for Native communities. The signage's framing of the Mound Path, and thus its re-storying of mounds and mound-building cultures, begins:

> Indigenous peoples have built gathering places and monuments across North America since our origins. Of these, the Mound Builder earthworks are the most significant land architecture. They rival the Giza pyramids and the Temple of the Sun in their scale and scientific value. The design of our campus translates ancestral mounds into steel, glass and landscape architecture.

The re-storying situates earthworks within broader Indigenous practices of creating places in the landscape both for communal gathering and for communal commemoration. Also, the re-storying makes comparisons to better-known—and highly valued—traditions of ancient large-scale construction, such as the pyramids in Egypt and Incan temple sites in Peru. Finally, the re-storying quickly links ancient Indigenous "land architecture"—building with rocks, clays, and soils—to a contemporary Indigenous "landscape architecture" that combines these earthen materials used for millennia with more recently introduced materials such as steel and glass. This linking is asserted not as natural or inevitable, but rather as accomplished through a deliberate process of "translation."

The signage's re-storying continues:

> The FAM Mound rises to a height of 90 feet as its circular shape recalls the movement of the sun across the sky. The FAM Mound honors Mound Builder cultures that thrived across North America from about 3500 BCE to 1751 CE. Many of the tribal nations in Oklahoma today descend from these cultures. For some communities, mounds remain prominent in ceremonial life.

Notice here the specific justification for the mound's circular shape, as well as the incorporation of specific dates. The use of 1751 as a significant end date is notable for its specificity, and it is likely to prompt many visitors to ask, "Why 1751?" This mid-eighteenth-century date falls long after the first known contacts with Europeans but before the American Revolution in 1776, the ratification of the United States Constitution in 1788, or the passage of

FIGURE 6. Signage framing the Mound Path at First Americans Museum. Photograph by Chadwick Allen.

the Indian Removal Act in 1830. Relatively few visitors are likely to know that 1751 is a date commonly used by archaeologists to mark the "end" of the so-called Mississippian mound-building culture—although, if visitors are paying careful attention, that information is available in other parts of the museum. The re-storying clearly links mound-building cultures associated with the period 3500 BCE to 1751 CE to contemporary Indigenous nations and to contemporary Indigenous practices.[35] This unequivocal linking of the Indigenous past to the Indigenous present is a pointed divergence from orthodox archaeological, historical, and museological accounts, which continue to rely on the discourses of "mystery" and "enigma" when describing what became of Indigenous mound-building cultures of the past.[36]

The signage's re-storying concludes:

> We invite you to take a journey of understanding to the top of the FAM Mound. In walking this path, you will deepen your appreciation for our cultures and the vitality of the land we call home.

The invitation to visitors links embodied encounter to the possibility of greater understanding. In addition, the invitation makes a set of subtle but bold assertions: one about the endurance of ancient Indigenous practices into the contemporary era, and one about contemporary Indigenous claims to what is now the U.S. settler state of Oklahoma, where so many Indigenous nations were forcibly removed or confined in the nineteenth century. This second assertion is all the more pointed if one is aware of the history of the specific lands and waters upon which the museum now stands, which were a grimy oilfield and toxic Superfund site in the recent past but, before that, a vibrant homeland to multiple Indigenous Peoples, including the Apache, Caddo, Tonkawa, and Wichita.[37]

To begin their ascent of the Mound Path's rising spiral, visitors exit the glass-and-steel Hall of The People, where they encountered the re-storying, and head north, toward the restored riverbank and the pathway's access point located at the eastern edge of the spiral's opening. As they move clockwise along the paved pathway, visitors are offered opportunities to enhance their "journey of understanding" through multiple types of signage, several of which provide QR codes so that those carrying smart-phones can "Learn More." This initial section of the outdoor pathway is integrated with components of the indoor museum facility (see figure 7). As they ascend east and south, visitors pass between the Hall of The People on their right (i.e., to the west), where they can look through the reinforced glass to see both the framing signage and the far side of the mound, including the tunnel marking the winter solstice, and, on their left (i.e., to the east), the indoor exhibit galleries. At one point, visitors can look through a window positioned above the main entrance to the museum; this view faces due east, aligning visitors to the dramatic stacked-stone Walls of Remembrance (commemorating those who perished during forced Removal), the central courtyard and Remembrance Gate, and, ultimately, to sunrise (see figure 8).

FIGURE 7. The first part of the Mound Path is integrated between the Hall of The People and the main exhibit building at First Americans Museum. Photograph by Chadwick Allen.

During this first part of the upward "journey," visitors are also offered three opportunities to pause for reflection as they pass three outdoor terraces integrated into the facility's larger structure: first, the Moon Terrace on their left (to the east), then the Sun Terrace on their right (to the west), and finally the Stars Terrace again on their left (to the east).[38] The first and third terraces create stylized oculi—the Moon Terrace with a narrow, distinctly eye-shaped sky opening, the Stars Terrace with a larger, more ovoid-shaped sky opening—while the second terrace invites visitors to view the sun's zenith and western descent through the stylized lens of the glass Hall of The People. Moreover, with the specific sequencing, visitors are encouraged to move from contemplation of their relations with our closest cosmic companion, the moon, to contemplation of their relations with our solar system's central, life-giving star, the sun, to contemplation of their relations

FIGURE 8. Visitors ascending the Mound Path can experience First Americans Museum's eastern alignments by looking through a window positioned over the museum's main entrance. Photograph by Chadwick Allen.

with the more distant galaxy, represented by the stars. The terraces are part of FAM's project of re-storying the mounds and mound-building cultures, helping to manifest our earthly relations with the broader cosmos. But it is notable that, of the three named cosmic entities, only the sun is reliably visible when the museum is open to visitors. The moon is occasionally visible during daylight hours, but not always, whereas the stars are rarely visible. The terraces, their signage, the information linked to their QR codes, and their purposeful sequencing, therefore, appear designed more for sparking visitors' imaginations than for offering actual cosmic encounters. In this way, responsibility for activating the site's assertions of these key relationships falls largely to visitors themselves.[39]

As they proceed beyond this first part of the Mound Path situated between the Hall of The People and the galleries, visitors encounter five additional, free-standing signs sited at regular intervals along the ascending spiral, which provide additional opportunities for enhancing their knowledge and engaging their imaginations. The signs are labeled The First Americans, Earthen Observatories, Ancestral Architecture, Indigenous by Design, and New Perspectives. I won't describe each in detail, but I want to emphasize that here, too, the sequencing is meant to be instructive, perhaps didactic, in shaping visitors' "journey of understanding" and in re-storying Indigenous mounds and mound-building cultures. The initial sign, labeled The First Americans, is positioned so that viewers face the interior circle of the Festival Plaza as they engage its text and images—this positioning holds for all but the final sign in the sequence (see figure 9). Ghosted behind the text and primary images on this first sign are ancient pottery designs; the specific motif is repeated throughout the museum and thus links the outdoor signage to the indoor galleries. The sign's text is notable for how it anchors ancient mound-building practices, which, in dominant discourses, are associated primarily with the Ohio and Mississippi valleys and the Southeast, to the lands that now form the contemporary settler state of Oklahoma—perhaps helping to justify the building of this new mound in Oklahoma in the twenty-first century. The text is notable, as well, for how it explicitly calls out the need for appropriate "ethical standards" when museums create and manage Indigenous collections.

FIGURE 9. The first sign posted further along the Mound Path is labeled The First Americans. Photograph by Chadwick Allen.

Arranged into four blocks, the text reads:

First American cultures were flourishing millennia before European arrival. Our ancestors engaged in cultural, scientific and economic exchange across thousands of miles.

Spiro was a key city during the Mississippian period of Mound Builders (900–1450 CE). The site was home to about 10,000 residents at its peak and anchored the Caddo region for more than 600 years.

Located in present-day eastern Oklahoma, Spiro is among the most important archaeological sites in North America.

Many tribal nations in Oklahoma today descend from Mound Builder cultures. Places like Spiro connect us with our ancestors. The looting that took place at Spiro and other ancestral sites has amplified the importance of ethical standards for museum collections.

FAM's assertions here directly counter more typical dominant accounts. As one relevant example, the Oklahoma History Society's webpage for the Spiro Mounds Archaeological Center currently describes the site not as a place of Indigenous connection but rather as a "Prehistoric Gateway and Present-day Enigma." The webpage asserts, as well, that "Much of the Spiro culture is still a mystery."[40]

The initial sign on the Mound Path juxtaposes its four-part re-storying text with a map of the eastern half of North America that details the expansive reach of Mississippian-era mound-building cultures—with the Spiro site in what is now eastern Oklahoma clearly marked at the map's western edge—and with an image of a beautifully engraved shell cup. Importantly, similar to the map, the featured artwork is not an ancient relic but rather a contemporary production. The caption states, "This engraved shell cup represents the ancient wisdom passed to us from our Mound Builder ancestors," but reveals that the work of intricate engraving on a full conch shell was created not hundreds or thousands of years ago but in 2020 by the artist Dan Townsend. Some viewers will be aware that Townsend is a well-known contemporary shell artist of Creek and Cherokee descent. Together, the signage, the map with its caption, and the image with its caption work to emphasize the museum's argument—what I am calling its re-storying—about Indigenous cultural continuity over long periods and despite violent dispossession and forced removal. Moreover, this argument continues across the sequence of the four signs that follow.[41] The sequence ends, at the ninety-foot summit of the mound, with the sign labeled New Perspectives, which orients visitors not to the Festival Plaza and the interior circle of the mound, but north toward the river and the land beyond. The sign's narration begins, "Take a moment to observe the expansive Southern Plains before you. Today more than 450,000 tribal citizens call Oklahoma home. We share this land with neighbors who have migrated from across the world to reside here." The sign's narration concludes, "The FAM mound is a place of connection and continuity. Its presence is an invitation to consider your relationship to the sky, this land and to others."

Mounds as Vital Life

The official FAM opening in September 2021 was scheduled on a Saturday so that a large number of people from near and far would have the opportunity to participate. All thirty-nine of Oklahoma's tribal nations sent representatives to walk in a grand entry, in which the nations processed through the museum building and the Hall of The People out onto the Festival Plaza. Following this grand procession, a presentation of colors by Native veterans, and an invocation by a Native spiritual leader, official remarks—full of passion and good humor—were delivered to a diverse and lively crowd gathered under the shade of a large marquee. Those in attendance heard from the museum's distinguished Kaw and Muscogee director, James Pepper Henry, the Osage (and first Native) Mayor of Oklahoma City, the Governor of the Chickasaw Nation, tribally enrolled members of the Oklahoma state legislature, and other local and state dignitaries. Guided tours, outdoor music performances, dancing, games for children, opportunities to sample updated versions of traditional foods at the museum's Arbor Café and Thirty-Nine Restaurant, and other activities were scheduled across the remainder of the day and weekend. It was an inspiring and joyful experience, although it was not an opportunity for peaceful contemplation of the facility's new mound.

Because my visit to Oklahoma had to be brief, before heading to the airport on Sunday I made sure to be back at the museum the minute its doors opened. Few others had yet to arrive so early in the morning, so I was able to spend a quiet hour with the new mound on my own. Since the paved pathway was not yet complete, I used my time to slowly walk the base of the spiraling embankment, tracing the circumference of the Festival Plaza in a clockwise arc, lingering at the trapezoidal entrance to the winter solstice tunnel and lingering again at the base of the angled, triangular slope of the ninety-foot summit.[42] Passing through the spiral's northern opening, I then walked west along a stretch of the restored riverbank, toward the city skyline, turning back to photograph the mound from additional angles and perspectives. As the sun rose higher in the eastern sky, its bright ball first refracted through and then balanced upon the soaring glass dome of the Hall of The People, I reentered the Festival Plaza and again walked its circumference, now counterclockwise. The spiraling mound has been planted with indigenous grasses and wildflowers, many of which were still in bloom in late September. In the quiet of the early morning, without the sensory distractions of the opening ceremony, it was clear that the mound itself was alive with movement and sound. A gentle breeze swayed the tall grasses and yellow sunflowers; small birds flitted in and out of intricately cast shadows; flying and crawling insects hummed, clicked, and buzzed in a teeming chorus (see figure 10). This life, this vibrant, other-than-human life, I reflected, is an integral component of the re-storying of the mound as physical site, of the re-storying of the mound as conceptual construct, and of the re-storying of our understandings of mound-building and mound-stewarding cultures. Part of the mound's compositional logic, this complex vitality is perhaps the mound's most profound message about the Indigenous present—and about possible Indigenous futures.[43]

When I visited FAM in March 2023 and was able to ascend the mound, I photographed a woolly caterpillar—a living symbol of transformation—inching its way across the paved pathway (see figure 11). Although spring grasses and flowers were only beginning to poke through the dormant winter grasses, there were signs of the mound's life all around. The subtle presence of butterflies and caterpillars at mound sites, whether ancient or newly

FIGURE 10. Sunflowers in bloom on the promontory mound at First Americans Museum. Photograph by Chadwick Allen.

FIGURE 11. A woolly caterpillar crosses the Mound Path at First Americans Museum. Photograph by Chadwick Allen.

constructed, reminds us of both the land's and the people's power to renew, adapt, change.[44] When Indigenous Peoples were forcibly removed from their mounded homelands in the nineteenth century, not only was access to their lands, waters, and skies taken from them but also their relations to the vibrant other-than-human creatures with whom they shared those lands, waters, and skies, as well as their relations to the ancestral forces that imbued those natural and built environments—forces made manifest in the movements of insects, birds, and animals and in the movements of wind, light, and water.

Part of what is so inspiring about the reactivation of large-scale earthworks construction and care at the tribally specific Chickasaw and Choctaw cultural centers and at the multitribal First Americans Museum is that, nearly two hundred years after forced removal, these structures represent an active transposition of ancient understandings of Indigenous power from the old Southeastern, Ohio Valley, and Mississippi Valley homelands to the new homelands in Oklahoma. These structures also represent a continuation of ancient citational practices in which diverse earthworks help connect contemporary individuals, families, communities, and nations to specific ancestors, to specific ancestral sites and sacred spaces, to specific ancestral events, as well as to specific ancestral ideas and practices. These new mounds help us ask sophisticated questions about forced migrations and Indigenous practices of place-making, including the marking of arrivals and the creation of origins. Over repeated visits to the First Americans Museum, I have come to think of the combination of the bustling highways and calm stretch of restored river, the rising spiral of the Mound Path teeming with life, and the dynamic solstice tunnel and promontory as not only embodying but also enacting precisely this: a new narrative of Indigenous emergence.

CHADWICK ALLEN is associate vice provost for faculty advancement and professor in the Department of English at the University of Washington.

References

Abercrombie, Stanley. 1984. *Architecture as Art: An Esthetic Analysis.* New York: Van Nostrand Reinhold Co.

Ahtone, Heather. 2019. "Considering Indigenous Aesthetics: A Non-Western Paradigm." *Newsletter for the American Society for Aesthetics* 39, no. 3 (Winter): 3–5.

Ahtone, Heather. 2022. "Shifting the Paradigm of Art History: A Multi-sited Indigenous Approach." In *The Routledge Companion to Indigenous Art Histories in the United States and Canada,* edited by Heather Igloliorte and Carla Taunton, 42–52. London: Routledge.

Allen, Chadwick. 2022. *Earthworks Rising: Mound Building in Native Literature and Arts.* Minneapolis: University of Minnesota Press.

Bevan, Robert. 2022. *Monumental Lies: Culture Wars and the Truth about the Past.* London: Verso.

De Botton, Alain. 2006. *The Architecture of Happiness.* New York: Pantheon.

Goeman, Mishuana. 2013. *Mark My Words: Native Women Mapping Our Nations.* Minneapolis: University of Minnesota Press.

Goldberger, Paul. 2022. *Why Architecture Matters.* Rev. ed. New Haven, CT: Yale University Press.

Grant, Elizabeth, Kelly Greenop, Albert L. Refiti, and Daniel J. Glenn, eds. 2018. *The Handbook of Contemporary Indigenous Architecture.* Singapore: Springer.

Howe, LeAnne. 2014. "Embodied Tribalography: Mound Building, Ball Games, and Native Endurance in the Southeast." *Studies in American Indian Literatures* 26, no. 2 (Summer): 75–93.

Howe, LeAnne, and Jim Wilson. 2015. "Life in a 21st Century Mound City." In *The World of Indigenous North America*, edited by Robert Warrior, 3—26. New York: Routledge.

Kahn, Andrea, and Carol J. Burns. 2021. "Why Site Matters." In *Site Matters: Strategies for Uncertainty through Planning and Design*, edited by Andrea Kahn and Carol J. Burns, 1—13. New York: Routledge.

Krinsky, Carol Herselle. 1996. *Contemporary Native American Architecture: Cultural Regeneration and Creativity*. New York: Oxford University Press.

LaVere, David. 2007. *Looting Spiro Mounds: An American King Tut's Tomb*. Norman: University of Oklahoma Press.

Malmar, Joy Monice, and Frank Vodvarka. 2013. *New Architecture on Indigenous Lands*. Minneapolis: University of Minnesota Press.

Meredith, America. 2016. "Those Who Are Above, Those Who Are on Earth: Effigy Mounds of Southern Wisconsin." *First American Art Magazine* 10 (Spring): 22—29.

Mignolo, Walter D. 2000. *Local Histories / Global Designs: Coloniality, Subaltern Knowledges, and Border Thinking*. Princeton, N.J.: Princeton University Press.

Nabokov, Peter, and Robert Easton. 1989. *Native American Architecture*. New York: Oxford University Press.

Nisbet, James. 2021. *Second Site*. Princeton, N.J.: Princeton University Press.

Page, Alison, and Paul Memmott. 2021. *Design: Building on Country*. First Knowledges series. Australia: Thames & Hudson.

Pearce, Margaret Wickens. 2014. "The Last Piece is You." *Cartographic Journal* 51, no. 2 (May): 107—22.

Pratt, Mary Louise. 1992. *Imperial Eyes: Travel Writing and Transculturation*. London: Routledge.

Pratt, Stacy. 2021."Dawning of a New Era: First Americans Museum Opens in Oklahoma City." *First American Art Magazine* 32 (Fall): 18—25.

Rifkin, Mark. 2017. *Beyond Settler Time: Temporal Sovereignty and Indigenous Self-Determination*. Durham, N.C.: Duke University Press.

Rigaud, Antonia. 2012. "Disorienting Geographies: Land Art and the American Myth of Discovery." *Miranda* 6: 1—16.

Notes

1. Author of the novels *Shell Shaker* and *Miko Kings*, the poetry collection *Evidence of Red*, the essay collection *Choctalking on Other Realities*, and the verse play *Savage Conversations*, Howe, originally from Ada, Oklahoma, is a distinguished professor of creative writing at the University of Georgia, where Wilson is also on the faculty. In 2014, Howe published the provocative essay "Embodied Tribalography: Mound Building, Ball Games, and Native Endurance in the Southeast." In 2015, when First Americans Museum was in an early phase of its construction (and then known as the American Indian Cultural Center and Museum [AICCM]), Howe and Wilson published the similarly provocative essay "Life in a 21st Century Mound City."

2. An example of a tribally-based publisher is the Chickasaw Press and its imprint White Dog Press, based in Ada, Oklahoma, the contemporary seat of government for the Chickasaw Nation.

3. First Americans Museum's innovative curation, for instance, is led by senior curator Heather Ahtone (Chickasaw), an accomplished art historian who has written extensively about the distinctiveness of Indigenous aesthetics. See Ahtone, "Considering Indigenous Aesthetics: A Non-Western Paradigm" and "Shifting the Paradigm of Art History: A Multi-sited Indigenous Approach."

4. The close proximity of these new earthworks to accessible, public sites for Indigenous-centered celebration, education, and tourism is significant, for it is one of several features that distinguish these contemporary Indigenous constructions from non-Native examples of twentieth- and twenty-first-century "earth art" or "land art," which are typically conceived as the vision of a single (non-Native) artist and typically constructed at a distance from any population center (Native or non-Native). The remoteness of these non-Native "art" works, and thus the difficulty of viewing or encountering them with any regularity, is part of their (non-Native) aesthetic appeal. As art historian Antonia Rigaud argues in her essay "Disorienting Geographies: Land Art and the American Myth of Discovery," "the major land artworks are positioned, by definition, far away. One has to get to them, as one would to some natural wonder" (7). Moreover, given the difficulty of physically viewing or engaging most major examples of earth art or land art, these non-Native works are known predominantly not as built environments or even as outdoor "sculpture" but rather as "traces in the shape of photographs, films or [other] accounts" (7). They are known, in other words, primarily through forms of visual or discursive mediation rather than through modes of direct sensory experience. A frequently cited example is Robert Smithson's celebrated *Spiral Jetty,* a land art sculpture constructed in Utah's Great Salt Lake, which is known to the majority of its admirers not through direct visual or physical encounter but rather through viewing a documentary film made during the work's construction in 1970 and various aerial photographs made over the subsequent five decades.

5. Consistent care and regular maintenance are other features that distinguish these Indigenous constructions from most non-Native examples of earth art and land art, which are often constructed without plans (or designated funds) for their upkeep. For an account of how these non-Native earth art sites change over time as they become overgrown with vegetation or as they weather, erode, degrade, suffer vandalism, and so forth, and for an argument for how to interpret such changes, see Nisbet, *Second Site.*

6. The Indian Removal Act was signed into law by U.S. President Andrew Jackson on May 28, 1830, and the forced removal of Southeastern and other Indigenous nations to the Indian Territory was conducted across the 1830s and 1840s. Through Presidential Proclamation 780, U.S. President Theodore Roosevelt brought Oklahoma into the union as the forty-sixth state on November 16, 1907.

7. I am borrowing the language of "historic places and commemorative landscapes" from Robert Bevan in *Monumental Lies: Culture Wars and the Truth about the Past,* 4.

8. There has been a significant shift from works like *Native American Architecture* (1989), written by non-Native anthropologist Peter Nabokov and non-Native architect Robert Easton, which focus primarily on "traditional" or "customary" forms of American Indian architectural design and building, to works like *Contemporary Native American Architecture: Cultural Regeneration and Creativity* (1996), written by non-Native architectural historian Carol Herselle Krinsky, which focus on "new" American Indian architectural designs that have been conceived and built since the 1960s. More recent texts that continue this focus on the "new" include the beautifully illustrated, North American-focused *New Architecture on Indigenous Lands,* written by non-Native architectural historians Joy Monice Malmar and Frank Vodvarka (2013), and the comprehensive, more globally focused compendium *The Handbook of Contemporary Indigenous Architecture,* edited by the international team of architects, architectural historians, and architectural anthropologists Elizabeth Grant, Kelly Greenop, Albert L. Refiti (Samoan), and Daniel J. Glenn (Crow) (2018). The scholarship continues to evolve in innovative ways. In Australia, for instance, the First Knowledges series published by Thames & Hudson includes the title *Design: Building on Country* (2021). Written by Indigenous Australian designer Alison Page (Walbanga and Wadi Wadi) and non-Native architect and anthropologist Paul Memmott, *Design* begins from the premise that "Country-focused design is an attempt to reinvigorate ancient conversations about the human connection to nature and how the built environment can play a vital part in this dialogue" (19).

9. In *Earthworks Rising,* I explore how twentieth- and twenty-first-century Indigenous writers, artists, and intellectuals engage ancient North American earthworks and, importantly, enduring earthworks principles in their contemporary productions—from works of visual and installation art produced in multiple media to works of alphabetic literature written in multiple genres to works of drama and other modes of performance embodied at multiple venues. Similar to the opening account of the solstice celebration at First Americans Museum, I narrate, as well, a personal history of encounters with extant mounds and participation in collaborative and embodied research alongside Native writers, artists, and intellectuals at multiple earthworks sites.

10. The large scale of these new earthworks is significant. As I note in *Earthworks Rising,* a number of anthropologists and tribal members affirm that, following forced Removal in the 1830s, small-scale, ceremonial mound building continued—and continues—in what is now Oklahoma. In contrast, large-scale building had already ceased prior to Removal. Not all contemporary Indigenous individuals and nations, however, agree that new mounds should be built—or that extant ancient mounds should be repaired or reconstructed. In a 2016 article about the thousands of ancient effigy mounds constructed in what is now southern Wisconsin, for example, Cherokee artist and intellectual America Meredith states, "Local tribes don't reconstruct the mounds," and she quotes a Ho-Chunk elder as stating, "The Ho-Chunk traditional courts say not to create new mounds" and "There is a reason they [the ancient builders] quit making mounds" (25, 27).

11. See Kahn and Burns, "Why Site Matters," 3.

12. Goldberger attributes the maxim to the distinguished non-Native art historian Vincent Scully.

13. I am borrowing the language of "compositional logic" from Abercrombie in *Architecture as Art: An Esthetic Analysis,* 120.

14. In *Earthworks Rising,* I describe "enduring earthworks principles" as including not only the principle of layering diverse materials in order to construct durable structures, but also the principle of creating multiple structural patterns, within individual mounds but especially among multiple mounds arranged into earthworks complexes and cities, and the principle of creating multiple simultaneous alignments. For example, aligning a mound to a river or other waterway, to a significant hill or natural ridge in the surrounding environment, to the movements of the sun, moon, or stars in the sky-world above, and to other constructed mounds and embankments, while also aligning the same mound to significant aspects of story, to social and political organization, to economics and trade, to ceremony, ritual, and other forms of spiritual practice. Moreover, I describe the principle of not only aligning but also encoding earthworks through the abstract language of mathematics. Finally, I describe the principle that earthworks can function as sites for Indigenous return and the principle that earthworks can embody story.

15. We might add here, too, Ahtone's account of the imposition of "Western knowledge paradigms and vocabularies" that separate "aesthetics, science, and religion" into "exclusive bodies of knowledge" and that therefore struggle to recognize Indigenous understandings of knowledge as "holistic" ("Considering Indigenous Aesthetics," 4).

16. I am drawing on Goldberger for these generalizations about architecture; see 30 (form of communication), 14 (simultaneously form and symbol), 16 (unifying social force), 72 (public presence), 101 (orienting device) and 117 (directional space). In *The Architecture of Happiness,* non-Native philosopher Alain de Botton makes the related point that "buildings *speak*" and that architecture is a "material articulation" of ideas and values (71, 72, 73).

17. The earthen structure at the Chickasaw Cultural Center is also described as a "minko" or "chief's" mound.

18. The Nanih Waiya is considered by Choctaw and other Southeastern peoples as the Mother Mound: a place of the people's emergence from the earth and, simultaneously, a place of the people's settlement after long migration. See Allen, *Earthworks Rising,* 364n14.

19. A third style or genre of new mounds built in Oklahoma—but originating in the twentieth century rather than the twenty-first—includes the Muscogee (Creek) Nation Mound Building, part of the Nation's Tribal Complex located in the town of Okmulgee, south of Tulsa. First constructed in 1974 and later renovated, this circular, earth-embanked contemporary structure is large enough to house both the legislative and judicial branches of the Muscogee government. The building's innovative, contemporary design is modeled after the reconstructed Ocmulgee Earth Lodge located in the Ocmulgee Mounds National Historical Park, part of the Muscogee's pre-Removal homelands in what is now

the state of Georgia. Muscogee (Mvskoke) geographer Laura Harjo describes earthworks as examples of what she calls "kin-space-time-envelopes" and she describes the Muscogee Nation Mound Building in terms of how it links contemporary governance to Indigenous sovereignty. See her contribution to the "Mound Summit" webinar hosted online by the Center for Native Futures on December 4, 2021, https://www.centerfornativefutures.org/moundsummit.

20. See https://www.chickasawculturalcenter.com/explore/chikasha-inchokka-traditional-village/.

21. Many cite Mark Rifkin's *Beyond Settler Time: Temporal Sovereignty and Indigenous Self-Determination,* although the issue has been engaged by a wide range of scholars.

22. See Allen, *Earthworks Rising,* 187–203, where I describe the center in detail and where I acknowledge my debt to Amanda Cobb-Greetham (Chickasaw), former administrator for the Chickasaw Nation's Division of History and Culture, who gave me a behind-the-scenes tour of the Chickasaw Cultural Center in 2013 and who engaged in extensive conversation with me about the center's design and potential for meaning-making.

23. As I draft this essay in 2023, the Chickasaw Nation is building a new resort facility adjacent to First Americans Museum.

24. The Choctaw Cultural Center includes a large and highly dynamic 3D scale model of the Moundville site inside its facility.

25. Rivers, of course, are the Indigenous superhighways of the past.

26. As noted on its website, First Americans Museum can also be described as situated at the "confluence of Interstates 35, 40, 235, and 44." See https://famok.org/about-us/.

27. See https://www.chickasawculturalcenter.com/visit/campus-map/.

28. See, for example, Pratt, *Imperial Eyes.*

29. On the coloniality of knowledge, see Mignolo, *Local Histories / Global Designs.*

30. For an extended analysis of this signage, see Allen, *Earthworks Rising,* 187–203.

31. This is also true for the Choctaw Cultural Center's ceremonial mound.

32. One of the most infamous cases of looting a major earthworks site happened to occur in eastern Oklahoma, at the Mississippian Spiro Mounds site located in what is now LeFlore County. See, for instance, LaVere, *Looting Spiro Mounds.*

33. I am grateful to James Pepper Henry for giving me a behind-the-scenes tour of First Americans Museum while it was still under construction.

34. As I relate in the conclusion to *Earthworks Rising,* I walked part of the promontory mound with James Pepper Henry in 2019. There was no paved pathway then, no guardrail, and no signage. It was a powerful experience, but necessarily different from the experience intended for subsequent visitors.

35. Notice, too, that the signage is careful not to disclose details about either historical or contemporary "ceremonial life."

36. See Allen, *Earthworks Rising.*

37. First Americans Museum includes a formal land acknowledgment on its website, which states, in part: "We honor the indigenous people who inhabited

these lands before the United States was established. They include the Apache, Caddo, Tonkawa, and Wichita. We also honor those tribes who have a historical relationship to this region, including the Comanche, Kiowa, Osage and Quapaw. We acknowledge the Muscogee (Creek) and Seminole who were once assigned the land upon which FAM resides." See https://famok.org/about-us/.

38. For a detailed map of First Americans Museum, see https://famok.org /visit/.

39. This explicit engagement of visitors' imaginations links First Americans Museum's project of re-storying mounds and mound-building cultures to what Seneca scholar Mishuana Goeman describes in *Mark My Words: Native Women Mapping Our Nations* as Indigenous "(re)mapping": "a powerful discursive discourse with material groundings" and "the labor Native authors and the communities they write within and about undertake, in the simultaneously metaphoric and material capacities of map making, to generate new possibilities" (3). FAM offers visitors the opportunity to create a new "map" of mounds and mound-building cultures, one that includes relations to the sky-world above. But for this multidimensional map to become manifest, visitors must not only pay attention to the site and its signage but also conceive and then incorporate these complex relations through their imaginations. In her essay "The Last Piece is You," Potawatomi cartographer Margaret Wickens Pearce describes a similar process for engaging Indigenous discursive or narrative maps as the reader's or listener's "responsibility," first, to "imagine, memorize and store a strong mental conception of the [discursively mapped] landscape," and then, second, to fully "activate and thus complete the map through direct [embodied] experience" of the landscape (119). Both the contours of the story and the corresponding contours of the land (and sky) are incorporated into the reader's or listener's body through their imagination.

40. See https://www.okhistory.org/sites/spiromounds.

41. The third sign in the sequence, labeled Ancestral Architecture, includes the following list of styles or genres of ancient earthworks, concluding with the FAM mound's own genre of "observational mound": "Some mounds are burial sites, while others were platforms for important structures. Effigy mounds recall serpents, panthers, birds, and other significant animals. Observational mounds afford a sweeping view, serving strategic and scientific ends." The fourth sign in the sequence, labeled Indigenous by Design, includes the statement: "*21st Century Mound Builders* describes the architectural design of the FAM campus. We draw on the wisdom of our ancestors to innovate forms of art, architecture and creative expression."

42. During the 2023 summer solstice celebration, I noticed that the trapezoidal opening for the winter solstice tunnel mimics the trapezoidal opening for a plains tipi. Yet another alignment embedded within the FAM mound's complex, explicitly multitribal design.

43. In *Architecture as Art,* Abercrombie argues that a building—and, I would add as a friendly amendment, any purposely built structure, including an Indigenous earthwork—is "most alive when it exhibits change," that is, "when the patterns of its shadows reflect the seasons, and when, over many years,

its weathering and staining occur so that we know they were expected and planned for" (166–67).

44. See Allen, *Earthworks Rising,* for discussion of the presence of butterflies and caterpillars at several ancient earthworks sites, such as Serpent Mound in southern Ohio (63, 65).

JEFF BERGLUND

"But Always My Thoughts Stay with Me, My Own Way": Intellectual and Creative Claims of Sovereignty by Indian Boarding School Students in *The Colored Land: A Navajo Indian Book, Written and Illustrated by Navajo Children* (1937)

Abstract

In 1937, Ruth K. Brandt, Supervisor of Elementary Education, in the federal Office of Indian Affairs, edited and published *The Colored Land: A Navajo Indian Book, Written and Illustrated by Navajo Children* with Scribner's Sons. Diné elementary school students from the Tohatchi Boarding School in New Mexico were the featured writers of much of the text with supporting illustrations composed by students from the Santa Fe Indian School. It was presented by its editors as evidence of the government's successful approach to assimilation through education. Situating their work within frameworks offered by contemporary Diné poets, I argue that these young children resisted acculturation and assimilationist efforts in the Reorganization Era by maintaining cultural values and traditions and even, in a few cases, issuing challenges to Western epistemologies and educational regimes. This early collection of published creative work by Diné writers and artists features undercurrents of resistance alongside literary and intellectual claims of sovereignty.

> *In the Navajo creation story, the holy people and the first woman established the principles of education through the transfer of cultural knowledge and understanding . . . In particular, education from a Navajo worldview embraces movement across the spectrum of space, time, and place.*
> —WENDY SHELLEY GREYEYES (DINÉ)

> *Within the context of the home and community, a child learns to develop her full potential as an individual and to harmonize that individuality with communal needs. This is done through a holistic system of education that teaches the child that all things in life are related.*
> —MANLEY BEGAY JR. (DINÉ)

> *I write from the core belief the word of our ancestors still reverberates in our present. It is a whisper in the grasses moving in all directions.*
> —ELIZABETH WOODY (DINÉ/WARM SPRINGS/WASCO/YAKAMA)

THE COLORED LAND: A NAVAJO INDIAN BOOK, Written and Illustrated by Navajo Children and edited by Ruth K. Brandt was published in 1937 by Charles Scribner's Sons, the New York-based publisher famous for having published Henry James, Edith Wharton, Ernest Hemingway, F. Scott Fitzgerald, and many others. While the publisher was established in 1846, its children's division was launched in 1934, just three years prior to the publication of *The Colored Land*. Ruth K. Brandt was the supervisor of elementary education in the Office of Indian Affairs at the time—this detail is positioned prominently on the book's title page. Previously, Brandt wrote primarily for government publications and forums such as *Indians at Work*, also disseminated by the Office of Indian Affairs, not a commercial publisher. While her name is listed on the title page, none of the nineteen student poems are attributed to individual named authors; the introduction identifies a boy named Chee who first expresses the wish to be a pony that gives rise to a collaborative brainstorm and the poem "If" included later in the book. Instead, the introduction identifies the authors simply as elementary students at the Tohatchi Boarding School in New Mexico. Readers do learn some of the names (but no other biographical details, including tribal identity) of several of the student artists who are sixth graders from the Santa Fe Indian School, an intertribal boarding school. The book also includes photographs of Diné people, most attributed to tourist photographers. When there are photographs of Diné students, some are simply identified as students at a different boarding school, "Chin Le." The book's nine drawings, twenty-three photographs, nineteen poems, and twenty-four descriptive prose passages, in addition to an introduction by the editor, make this a polyvocal text that was most likely assembled by the editor and/or publisher.

While editing *The Diné Reader: An Anthology of Navajo Literature* my coeditors and I were looking for documentation of the first published writing in English by Diné writers.[1] In our introduction, we mentioned the anonymous, unnamed writers in this book, perhaps being the very first published Diné poets working in English: "Little did these early writers know that their writing would begin the legacy of written Diné literature and poetics. All of the voices in *The Diné Reader: An Anthology of Navajo Literature* are symbolically united in a refusal to forget the powerful, creative intelligence of the unnamed child poets who began the rich and unforgettable legacy of a written Diné literature" (Belin et al. 2021, 5). We acknowledged the brilliance of the unnamed poet or poets but only briefly paused to dwell on this masterful evidence of survival and resistance. In the introduction we also recognized the complicated legacy of boarding schools and instruction in English. We mentioned the writing by students at the Intermountain School in the 1950s through the 1970s (see King et al. 2021), as well as writing by students at the Santa Fe Indian School and the Institute for American Indian Arts in the 1960s through the early 1970s. My analysis here of *The Colored Land* follows from this much bigger project of thinking about the long trajectory of Diné and Southwestern Indigenous creative expressive arts aimed at public audiences.

The Colored Land is a text with many voices and different forms of expression at play. It is hardly a bilingual work, as only one word in Diné bizaad, the Navajo language, is used with frequency: "hogan."[2] I find deep meaning in this word's presence and other undercurrents of the value of home and family and place, a deep valuation of K'é and an understanding that ontologies and epistemologies emanate from culture and land. *The Colored Land* provides insights into the complexity and artistry of young minds in the precarious and estranging contexts of boarding schools in an era when the U.S. government was pushing Reorganization policies (the Navajo Nation rejected the Wheeler-Howard Act in 1934), and educators in government-sponsored schools for Native children were encouraging their fellow educators to employ culturally relevant materials in their pedagogy and curriculum design. This is a remarkable and strange text warranting deeper meditation and exploration, as it played a complex role in government propaganda efforts. At the same time, throughout the work, there are powerful claims about culture, thus the work also documents and preserves the ways that young children resisted acculturation and assimilationist efforts by describing cultural traditions and values. The title of this article borrows two powerful lines from "My Thinking," the last poem in the book, "But always my thoughts stay with me/ My own way" (Brandt 1937, 80). These lines condense and affirm what has been implicit throughout many of the poems: that the students issue expressions of intellectual and epistemological sovereignty, and even, in a few cases, offer overt critiques and challenges to Western knowledge and educational regimes.

Much has been written and studied about boarding schools. The project of collecting and examining student writing produced at these schools has answered the call of K. Tsianina Lomawaima (her own Msvkoke father attended the Chilocco boarding school), when she asked: "What has become of the thousands of Indian voices that spoke the breath of boarding school life?" (1994, xii).[3] No in-depth attention has been paid to Diné student writing *at* boarding schools until *Returning Home: Diné Creative Works from the Intermountain Indian School* (2021), which foregrounds the work of Diné student writers in the 1950s and beyond. The writing in *The Colored Land* predates by several decades the work included in *Returning Home*. Farina King, one of its editors, had previously and briefly focused on Diné student work produced at Crownpoint Boarding School from the late 1930s and from The Old Leupp Boarding School in the 1960s in her groundbreaking *Earth Memory Compass: Diné Landscapes and Education in the Twentieth Century* (2018). Of vital importance to my work here is King's concept of the "earth memory compass," which represents "a system of knowledge and epistemologies based on collective memories, values of the earth, and ties between peoplehood and the land" (King 2018, 5) and provides for Diné students the continuance of cultural values and knowledge.

The Tohatchi Boarding School was established in 1904, twenty-five years after the founding of the first federally funded off-reservation Indian boarding school: the Carlisle Indian Industrial School. The first U.S. government-sponsored boarding school on what is now the Navajo Nation was built in 1883 in Fort Defiance, only four years after Carlisle (Donovan); since 1869, a day school had existed on this site. In 1898, the Blue Canyon School, near Tuba City, was founded, and this became the Western Navajo School in 1904, and eventually the Tuba City Boarding School, which is still in operation today. By 1925, twelve years before the publication of *The Colored Land,* nine more had been built, including schools in the vicinity of Tohatchi, in Shiprock, New Mexico (1903); Chinle, Arizona (1910); and Toadalena, New Mexico (1914) (Greyeyes 2022, 180). In 1933, nearly "5000 Diné youth went to schools" out of the "approximately 13,000 Diné children [who] were eligible to matriculate" (King 2018, 77). During the late 1920s, and continuing after the Indian Reorganization Vote in 1934, the U.S. government began to emphasize Indigenous cultures and subject matter within the English-language curriculum. John Collier's 1933 "Indian New Deal" may have appeared, King argues, to "support Diné sovereignty as an Indigenous nation, [but] Collier and his partners used schools for a governmental agenda to modernize Diné society and to transform their relationship with Diné Bikéyah" (King 2018, 84).[4] It is against this social and political backdrop that Ruth K. Brandt's project was conceived, produced, and delivered, using the contributions of Diné elementary students at Tohatchi and sixth graders at the Santa Fe Indian School.

The Colored Land's publication precedes the better-known bilingual English and Diné bizaad readers such as *Little Herder in Autumn/'Aak'eedgo Na'niłkaadí Yázhi* (1940) and three others published in 1940, featuring English text written by non-Diné author Ann Clark, with Navajo text/ orthography by John Harrington, Robert Young, and William Morgan (Diné) with consultation by anthropologist-novelist, Oliver LaFarge, in some cases, and brilliant illustrations by Hoke Denetsosie (Diné).[5] The Education Division of the United States Office of Indian Affairs published them. Rebecca Benes and Peter Iverson both argue that these bilingual books served Commissioner Collier's administrative and educational goals (1933–1945), which would in turn build a foundation for implementing other policies that intended to reformulate Navajo governance and Navajos' relationships to their lands (Benes 2004, 57; and Iverson, 2002, 173).

In contrast to these commissioned books, Ruth K. Brandt, the editor of *The Colored Land,* and supervisor of elementary education, in the federal government's Office of Indian Affairs, was deeply interested in having Native students create their own readers and produce some of the materials that would be used in schools. In an article in *Indians at Work* from June 1935, Brandt writes about the disconnect between most teaching materials and the contexts with which Indigenous children are familiar and knowledgeable:

> This situation has necessitated developing our own reading in the classroom based directly on the accumulated speaking vocabulary of children and dealing with ideas gained through their personal experiences. The children as a group construct the material deciding what shall be included and how it should be stated . . . The children enjoy illustrating their own stories each in accordance with his own ideas and his artistic ability. (Brandt 1935, 25)

Despite these claims about producing work that values Diné children and delights and engages them, the book nonetheless serves the public role of propaganda in demonstrating the success of so-called assimilationist efforts: in this case, achievement of a successful facility with the English language and the documentation of how literature, art, and culture have been harnessed in this effort.

In her introduction to *The Colored Land* Brandt never mentions or identifies the traumatic impact of family separation and the difficulty children faced when living and studying within institutions that prioritized different values and epistemologies. Indeed, there are cringe-inducing and culturally myopic lines that suggest the school has stepped into the roles that children's families once occupied: "The development of the poems was not so much a method as it was a way of day by day living with children and sharing their thoughts; living with them as a mother lives with her children in the perfect freedom of mutual and sympathetic understanding. Only in such an atmosphere of complete confidence and happiness could these poems have come to be" (Brandt 1937, 6). There's no denying in this comment the willful invention of the experience of Diné students and their teachers at boarding school, young children who are studying and living away from their families, working in English and being taught systems of knowledge that rupture relationalities, the priority of K'é, and kinships of multiple sorts including relations with the land and the intimate knowledge conveyed by and within Diné bizaad about such things. Their teachers were hardly replacements for their mothers. Even the book's photographs of Diné women with children (one is by Frashers Studio, the other is unattributed) remind readers that these children have loving mothers and are in no need of surrogates (Brandt 1937, 21 and 23). While the book includes no photographs of teachers, these photographs of Diné mothers—smiling, dressed in a velveteen blouse with silver and turquoise, hair in a tsiiyééł— issue a powerful reminder to readers of the students' mothers from whom they have been separated.[6]

The photographs are presumably included in the service of authenticity, a major driver of the book's claims more generally, despite occasional editorial disruptions that remind readers that curatorial shaping and control may have molded if not distorted truths—as in the comments about motherly teachers. Brandt's introduction notes: "The pages of this book give an authentic and fairly comprehensive view of the Navajo country and of Navajo life, essentially as seen through the eyes of Navajo children. The need for having in written form an expression of their own pulsing thoughts and feelings and living experience gives zest to the efforts of the children in creating their own books" (Brandt 1937, 5). In a footnote below the table of contents, the editor offers a further gesture of authenticity: "Grateful acknowledgment is made to John Charles, Hazel Litzin and Tom Dodge, Navajos, for constructive suggestions; to Gle Has Bah Becenti, a Navajo grandmother, on bread-making; and to the Navajo children and their teachers for the text and photographs of school life" (Brandt 1937, 3). Within the pages of the book, a prose section identifies by name Day-E-Bize (The Horned One's Son), a Hatááłii, or healing singer, and elder educated in spiritual and cultural knowledge systems who visited the children to tell them stories (59). These references allow Brandt the opportunity to suggest that Diné adults are involved in shaping the curriculum of the school.

In 1935, Brandt had already included such student writing in *Indians at Work*—an essay on Navajo weddings by Cora Ben Gould Yazzie, a fifth grader from the Toadlena Boarding School—to illustrate the ways that Native-focused topicality was supporting student development (Yazzie 1935). And, one year before *The Colored Land* was published, eleven poems written by Navajo students at Tohatchi were included in Office of Indian Affairs 1936, 15–16.[7] Brandt is not named in this special issue. Seven of these eleven poems produced by students working with Miss Evangeline Dethman, grouped under the heading, "Navajo Group Poetry," were later included in *The Colored Land* with few changes other than commas in place of dashes. "If I Were a Pony" was the most edited with a title change to "If," and with two significant changes to wording, one to avoid repetition and the other to improve rhythm, raising some further questions about editorial intervention/meddling of the book edited by Ruth K. Brandt published in 1937. Two Navajo students working with Dethman at Tohatchi were identified by first name—Sallie and Ray—which is noteworthy since author's names were infrequently included in *The Colored Land*.

Within the colonial framework of the boarding school—refashioned in the 1930s to educate "Indians" with culturally relevant material—the Office of Indian Affairs was able to publicize to American readers that their efforts were succeeding insofar as the students demonstrated their abilities to write in English. The editor positions the students as authorities and as transmitters of cultural knowledge, highlighting their creativity and talent. Their literary production is collective, which is unique in its resistance to individualist notions of authorship expected and commonplace in the twentieth century; but it is also indicative of a paternalistic and homogenizing view toward young students, and especially toward Indigenous Peoples and their representation in media, oriented commercially toward tourists who were led to believe that all Navajo people are the same.

The authorship of the poetry in the book *was* collaborative, if we are to believe Ruth Brandt's explanation about how poems came into being:

> Miss Dethman being highly sensitive to the artistic possibilities in children's expression, they likewise developed a surprising awareness of creative potentialities in situations, a frequent conclusion being, 'That would make a good poem,' or a suggestion, 'Let's make a poem about it.' Ideas recorded as expressed by the children were then submitted to rigorous group criticism. One child might suggest a more suitable work; one would drop a superfluous word, another would add a line, yet another might suggest a re-arrangement of the lines. Thus they worked until they were agreed that they had said what they wanted to say in the way in which they wished it said. (1937, 6)

This explanation is in keeping with Brandt's commentary in the 1935 entry in *Indians at Work* previously cited. While the poems are collaborative and the authors are never identified by name, Brandt's introduction glosses a few of the poem's origin stories, mentioning in one example the first name of one writer, Chee. Further creating some ambiguity is that the speaker's voice is cast in first-person—a choice of convention, perhaps, rather than singularity of voice.[8] While artists' names, from a different intertribal boarding school, *are* included, we have no details about any collaboration or brainstorming among artists or between writers and artists. It is unlikely that any dialogue occurred because of great distance and logistical inconveniences. All that Brandt offers is this: "As their vigorous paintings indicate, these children seem unerringly to have felt the true significance of the poems they chose to illustrate" (1937, 8).

The book's contents highlight Navajo life and emphasize aspects of cultural traditions, as well as experiences of children at boarding school. The nine illustrations are almost all attributed to individuals, sixth-grade students who were actually at the Santa Fe Indian School, whose art program, by the mid-1930s was headed by Dorothy Dunn. According to reflections in *One House, One Voice, One Heart: Native American Education at the Santa Fe Indian School,* she considered herself a "'guide,' asking her students questions about village life, and urging them to paint scenes from memory" (Hyer 2004, 44). How this collaboration came to be is not shared with readers of *The Colored Land.* Most of the illustrations accompany poems, so we might conclude that poetry was presented to student artists, and they picked their subject. While names are provided in most instances (seven out of the nine illustrations are attributed to individuals), they alone don't automatically signal tribal affiliation, and this creates some further dissonance with the work's subtitle. Of the artists' names mentioned, only one in particular, Chee, is a common Diné last name. The others are: Claude Nix, Quincy Tolloma, G. Smith & Thomas Thompson, Elias Montoya, W.H. Chee, Joe Leakity, and Joe Vigil. The only other possible noted tribal affiliation is made on the very first illustration of three men dancing attributed to Claude Nix, followed by the words "Cherokee, Talequah, Okla" (Brandt 1937, 4). In its placement, this illustration is not tied to any specific poem, although perhaps it could be aligned with a later prose section on Navajo Games and Dances as the men's moccasins include Diné designs—a raincloud and a whirling log. It is tempting to highlight the intercultural communication that occurred among students at both boarding schools and to make claims for potential intertribal creative expression across mediums, but so little is known about the process of assigning Santa Fe Indian School student artists to create art for accompanying poems, and even less about the involvement of students at Tohatchi in assembling the final product and matching works to their formal placement, that I am reluctant to draw greater conclusions about the dialogic and collaborative nature of the process than the meanings the published text itself affords in the interaction of the visual and written elements.

The photographs are primarily attributed to two commercial photographers: the California-based Frashers Studio and Gallup, New Mexico-based Mullarky Studios. Eight are from Frashers Studio; three are from Mullarky Studios. The additional twelve are unattributed to photographers, and, of those, five seem to have been taken in school contexts with a photographer supplied by the school or teacher. The photographs are typical products of the era, documenting the arcana of Navajo life for the public at large (Faris 2004, 159). Given the absence of the now common practice of citing permissions, it is likely that the editor and publishers pulled from this publicly available archive of photographs. The majority of those included fall into what James Faris calls "canons of realism" (2004, 17). The photographs serve the ethnographic and anthropologic function of the book. That individuals are not identified at all is unsurprising given the way photography operated to construct a monolithic, homogenized version of Navajo people—one woman interchangeable with another, for example. Inclusion of the photographs serves as a reminder of the *constructed* nature of the entire text, something produced to present a version of Navajo-ness. Photographs by Mullarkey and Frasher include images of children, sheep, chickens, a mother with a child in a cradleboard (see figure 1), a mother with children on a horse, a silversmith, sheep shearing, women weaving, women making bread, a family outside of a hogan, a summer home, the monolith, and Shiprock. A photograph of Day-E-Bize (previously mentioned) is placed next to a description of him. Later, in sections on hogan building and bread making, there are photographs, unattributed to anyone, featuring students in classrooms making hogans and making women and children making bread. The photographs, and to a lesser extent the prose sections, corroborate with "evidence" what Navajo people look like and the routines in which they are engaged. The poems and some of the drawings, by contrast, offer readers greater subtext, nuance, and multiple, simultaneous levels of meaning. The poems, in particular, offer traces of implied insights that readers almost ninety years hence can decode.

Before I turn to the specific content of *The Colored Land,* especially the poetry, I want to foreground how my interpretation is informed by thinking about space, place, land, memory, and poetry in the works of contemporary Diné poets Jake Skeets, Esther Belin, Sherwin Bitsui, and Elizabeth Woody. According to Skeets (2020), "Spatial contexts are centered in almost all ways of being within the Diné universe. There is order, and that order comes from a deep reverence for space." Similarly, in an essay, "Poem Making as Space Making," reflecting on Luci Tapahonso's poem, "That American Flag," Belin considers that "the practice of poem making is the study of creating space. Meaning (content). Placement (order). Aesthetic (Diné nishłi). What I mean is—the motion of making space—rearranges the sequential ebb and flow, ever so gradually creating beauty, before, behind, below, above" (2019, 343). Bitsui also joins this dialogue when he notes, "And that is the other kind of poetic I have access to, an ancient poetry that comes from the soil, comes from the land. This is brought to a kind of quality that resonates with language, somehow becoming the voice of the land. Language is another kind of landscape, an extension that goes away like the mist or the air that you breathe" (387). Bitsui's characterization of the ever-present vibration of

FIGURE 1. "The Navajo Woman" from *The Colored Land.*

words in the landscape is something that Elizabeth Woody (Diné) alludes to as well in one of the epigraphs to this article: "I write from the core belief the word of our ancestors still reverberates in our present. It is a whisper in the grasses moving in all directions." The work of the young poets of Tohatchi drew from the legacy of words alive in the landscape and it is in their resonantly powerful words that the meaning and beauty of the land survives and is passed on to us.

In what follows, I consider the ways that different poems make space and access the memory field that comes from the knowledge of the land and place. The confluence here between the Diné poetic theory and what Farina King terms "the earth memory compass" is remarkable; her metaphor is a means of condensing the ways that cultural memory and knowledge offers a wellspring to draw from. For the students, poetry is one way of reflecting on, of negotiating, and of reinvigorating their connection to knowledge and to place through language and creative form.

Much of the poetry in *The Colored Land* is simple in structure, employing clichés, or familiar rhetorical or literary conventions. I've come to see the poetry—especially read collectively, accruing depth when studied intertextually—as advancing complexities. The wisdom and the artistry are apparent if one reads subtextually, between the lines, and for the cultural allusions or reference points that abound. Consider the first two poems, printed on the same page: "My Home" and "This Land Is for Me" which thematically resonate with the book's title and serve as a frame for the reading of each successive poem:

> Navajo land
> With much room.
> The land is wide,
> The land is big.
> I like the land
> With lots of room. (Brandt 1937, 10)

This poem lays out the importance of being in Dinétah specifically and, if not, a reverence for this place—"I like the land" is the closest the speaker comes to such a claim—a recognition of its value and its expansiveness. In this six-line poem, "land" is repeated four times, "room" twice, and "wide" and "big" are additional descriptors, capaciousness and the freedom and openness it signifies are seen as the powerful value of Navajo land. The following page includes the second painting/illustration in the book, and includes the subtitle "The Land is Wide" (see figure 2). The artist Quincy Tolloma placed a young man in the left foreground, styled him with a headscarf, moccasins, a blouselike shirt, a concho belt, his hair in tsiiyéeł, and carrying a rope and bridle. Presumably, he's heading out to one of the three horses in the canyon distance with mesas further beyond. Arcing over the whole are two lines in blue and red, leading to the figurative sun in the upper right quadrant. These colors are associated with the sun's creation in Diné cosmology, when it was first created by First Man and First Woman out of stones, given horns that store male lightning and male thunder, and then fixed in the sky by darts of lightning (which may also explain the artist's rendering of some thin, jagged lines in the sky). The sun emanates heat rays and now moves across the sky in an arc because Jóhonaa'áí agreed to enter it and enervate it so it would move across the sky. Given the iconography of the wide-open land and sky to match, this young man is working to bring a horse or horses back from grazing as the sun continues its path through the later part of the afternoon. While we have little means of knowing what Tolloma thought of the poem, or whether he was inspired by it, or his own experiences, the collaboration over a distance between students at two different boarding schools

THE LAND IS WIDE

FIGURE 2. "The Land Is Wide" from *The Colored Land*.

produces deeper, more significant meaning than either text alone. The context of the painting in the book further deepens its subtext and allows it, too, to offer a rebuke of assimilationist efforts. Reading the poem and illustration together, it is impossible not to note the irony of students studying away from home in the confines of the boarding school (still on Navajo land in this case, but in a foreign institution), finding value and a sense of home within the wide-open Navajo homelands. With this recognition, its title is a powerful statement: *all of Dinétah is my homeland.*

The second poem, "This Land for Me," extends this preference through comparison and the introduction of the complex word for home, "hogan":

> It would be fun to travel
> Far across the sea.
> But my hogan's in Navajo land,
> It is the land for me. (Brandt 1937, 10)

There are no specific comments made about other traumatic and violent forced removals or their own displacement from home to boarding school; instead, there is an acknowledgment that while other places might be entertaining, they will never be home. The poem doesn't discuss how the Diné came to be in this place, what challenges were faced within the previous seventy-five years, or the explicit wisdom that emanates from this place. The last two lines of this simple four-line poem condense powerful and deep knowledge: "But my hogan's in Navajo land,/ It is the land for me." The end rhymes of line two and line four further reinforce the concluding message. Reading across both poems, and drawing attention to the possessive adjective, "my" in the title phrase "My Home" and in the phrase "my hogan," as well as the adjectival possessive clause "for me," readers come to understand the deeply personal commitment to and imbrication *in* and *with* place.[9] Both poems recycle elements of patriotic songs: "America the Beautiful" and "God Bless America" in the former song's reference to "spacious skies" and the later 1918 version's opening lines, "far across the sea."[10]

The third line's reference to "my hogan" being in Navajo land bears some further analysis. "Hooghan," anglicized to "hogan," is the only word in Diné bizaad to be used in any of the book's poems; by this time, "hogan" had become more familiar in the English lexicon in ways that parallel borrowed Indigenous terms made their way into English—"tipi," "canoe," "moose," "moccasin," as well as many others. Diné knowledge-holders and scholars have analyzed the way that this incorporation into English flattened the meaning of "hogan," reducing it simply to a word for a home dwelling or structure. Nonetheless, its deep, multivalent meaning would have resonated and been available through the students' "land memory compass." Elsewhere in *The Colored Land,* prose sections convey to readers some of the seemingly perfunctory elements of the built structures of hogans: for example, "The one in the picture is made of logs" or "Some homes are made of mud and stones" (Brandt 1937, 20). Photographs later in the book reference summer hogans (1937, 35) as well as structures built by students inside a classroom (see figures 3 and 4) and outside on school grounds at the Chinle Boarding School (69–73).[11] The description in the section on "The Navajo Family" also includes deep references to culturally resonant and symbolic aspects of hogans that extend an understanding of "hogan" well beyond structural elements: "The door of the hogan is always in the East. This is so that it looks toward the rising sun"; "There is a fire in the center of the hogan. This keeps the family warm. There is a smoke hole in top of the hogan" (20).

Diné archaeologist Kerry Thompson has spent years researching the cultural history and archaeological record of Diné hooghans, and has powerfully centered Diné teachings about the expansive epistemologies and cosmologies that frame thinking about the relationship of individuals within the universe. Diné holy people created a world for the humans, establishing boundaries

Here are the boys working on the logs.

FIGURE 3. "Here are the boys working on the logs" from *The Colored Land.*

Here we are having our teaparty. The furniture was too big
to go inside the hogan.

FIGURE 4. "Here we are having our teaparty" from *The Colored Land.*

within/encompassing six sacred mountains with directional teachings that map the movement of the day, year, and lifecycles and that have parallels with human thinking and action. In this way, the hogan is figurative for all Dinétah. Thompson writes, "Likewise, the earth, the sky, and the four sacred mountains compose a hogan that contains within it the Navajo universe" (Thompson 2009, 99) and "it is a sacred space in the sense that it is the physical locus from which one pursues hózhó in everyday life" (106).

The students' reference to the central fire, the central opening for the smoke's exit, the structure keeping the family dry and safe, the eastward facing door, the earth on which families sleep, all serve as reminders of the cardinal directions, of their associated sacred mountains, and their protection by father sky and mother earth. This is the original space-making that parallels what Belin above argues is the poetic act of making space: meaning, placing, and the aesthetic. In a later poem, "At Home at Night," students reflect on the cycle of the day: "I saw the sun rise this morning/I herded sheep all day" (Brandt 1937, 42). The poem's second stanza concludes with the following lines, taking the day (and life cycle of raising sheep) full circle:

> The sheep are in the corral now,
> The mutton is on the fire,
> Mother is making fried bread
> And oh, I am so tired! (Brandt 1937, 42)

Written at school, away from home, the students' work poignantly captures the long days of work and relief upon the close of day, safely penning up the sheep, and looking forward to a meal of mutton and fry bread prepared by the mother. While the speaker notes there was no time to play, filled with obligations, it is a full day, and the circle is complete for now. They are satisfied, fulfilled, where they are supposed to be: at home with their family, not at school, writing poems.

This poem's focus on the goodness of home expresses feelings similar to those expressed in later writing by Diné writers about the boarding school experience, including Laura Tohe's transcription of her grandmother Julia's story in *No Parole Today:* "It was good to get home, good to see my mother and all the ones at home. It was good to be home" (1999, xvi). Later, in Tohe's book, in a fictionalized story set at a later time, the narrator contemplates all that home and life means to her, from the vantage point of boarding school: "I'm lying on my bunk bed and thinking about home . . . I'm thinking about tall straight pine trees and the cool breeze that drifts from the mountain. I'm thinking about the smell of sage after a summer rain. I'm thinking of mom's warm, round tortillas" (Tohe 1999, 29). I cite this later work, much more well-known and more complexly developed, to highlight the ways this 1937 poem represents the power of writing to re-create home in the mind as a resource, if not recourse, to manage the emotional experience of longing and sorrow during separation of families while children were at boarding school.[12] This simple poem speaks volumes about Diné children's recognition of the goodness of family life and what was missing at school.

There are numerous moments in *The Colored Land* that emphasize the connection between the human and animal and physical world of the environment, including the two-line poem "Clouds": "The clouds go by,/The sheep of the sky" (Brandt 1937, 32). A beautiful illustration by G. Smith and Thomas Thompson (see figure 5) accompanies the poem and meaningfully reinforces the metaphoric association between clouds and sheep, with sheep being herded by a Navajo man or boy with a staff, dressed in moccasins, a concho belt, and wearing a headband, and sheep-like clouds hovering above. The skyworld mirrors the earthworld. They are parallel, but different, and in relationship with one another. The sixth-grade artists in Santa Fe clearly understood the brief poem written by elementary students in Tohatchi. Their image provides support for the analogy. In the

THE CLOUDS GO BY

FIGURE 5. "The Clouds Go By" from *The Colored Land*.

poem, metaphor, rhyme, and meter come together to offer this everyday and yet creative association; here, the poet/creator shepherds words and recognizes that the sheep of the sky have no minders, wandering by. Just as the sheep provide nourishment and the raw material for weaving that provides warmth and cover, the clouds provide shade and often rain and snow, other forms of nourishment. Diné people have long held sheep to be equally central, leading some to form, twenty-seven years ago, the organization, Dibé be' iiná, where their English slogan is "Sheep Is Life." This simple poem is all the more powerful when considering the socio-political and economic context in which it was written: a period of federally mandated livestock reduction when families were stripped of their livelihood (Roessel, 1974).

Readers also learn of the value of sheep and the hard work that comes with tending them; this also extends to the book's attention to weaving in poetry, drawings, prose sections, and photographs. *The Colored Land* explicitly references Navajo weaving and rugs throughout the book, not surprisingly featuring several photographs of women shearing sheep and of women sitting by their looms. In the short paragraph preceding the section "The Navajo Family," the editors of the book note, "The weaving of rugs is very important work for the Navajos, so there is a good deal about it in the stories and poems that the children write" (Brandt 1937, 17). In the section, "Navajo Women," written by the children, they write "Navajo women make rugs" (21). The poem "Wool Gathering" emphasizes hard work overtly: "I try to look busy/ Not full of sleep./ But in my thoughts/ I'm herding sheep" (21). While this may relate to the processing of wool after shearing for sale or in preparation for weaving, it may also offer a figurative commentary on engagement at school (its own type of wool gathering) where one may be lost in thought, sleepily imagining they're herding sheep. The poem, "A Rug," and its accompanying unattributed illustration (see figure 6) offers this association in powerful ways. First, the poem:

I herd the sheep.
I shear the sheep.
I spin and card the wool.
The rug I make,
Much time I take
To make my rug. (18)

This poem takes us through part of the sustained process of creating a rug. The repetition of the first-person pronoun in the first five lines of this sixth-line poem emphasizes the actor but also the actions through the subject-verb pairing in the first half: "I herd," "I shear," "I spin and card." The last line repeats the verb "make" and emphasizes that the work and designing produce "my" rug, the personal pronoun adjective emphasizing that this is the culmination of one weaver. The poem's only rhyming lines, line 4 and line 5, equally numbered in syllables and meter, emphasize the contemplation, labor, and forethought required of weavers: "The rug I make,/ Much time I take." When readers flip the page from 19 to 20, they see a beautiful illustration of one woman weaving on a loom and two others adjacent to her, carding and spinning wool. It appears the women's hair is styled in a tsiiyééł, and they are wearing long skirts and blouses, necklaces, and earrings with turquoise. The pattern of the rug appears indeterminant, but the other features of the loom that match photographs from this era include a tied-on upper beam, a tension bar, a loom bar, the warp, and a batten. The unnamed sixth-grade artist from the Santa Fe Indian School carefully portrays the women working at various stages of the process. The details of the women's clothing and the accuracy of the loom's construction, in particular, suggest some prior knowledge of Diné culture and traditions. For readers unfamiliar with rug weaving, the illustration supports and deepens the meaning of the poem.

THE RUG I MAKE

FIGURE 6. "The Rug I Make" from *The Colored Land*.

In a fictional story in this section that features a young Navajo girl named Tasbah, readers learn about even more of the steps required to prepare to make a rug, including the construction of the loom. After this detailed explanation, readers learn: "Tasbah's mother has no pattern to follow. All winter she has been thinking of the rug. She has made a picture of it in her mind. When the beautiful rug is finished it goes to the trader to be sold" (38–40).

The story is accompanied by two Frasher photographs: in the first, two women shear a sheep (37), and then, midway through the story above, another photograph depicts one woman using a spindle and sitting in front of a rug on a loom, the rug featuring a long-existing whirling log design (39) that would fall out of practice shortly after the publication of the book in the aftermath of World War II. This was because of its resemblance to the "swastika" associated with Nazis. After the story concludes, there is another photograph (this one by Mullarky Studios) of a woman weaving with a young boy sitting nearby. As in the poem, this passage emphasizes Tasbah's mother's attention to process, the ways that Tasbah is learning from her mother, and the structure and order of the life cycle of making a rug. While there are no details about how the process of weaving links to vital elements of Diné cosmology and philosophy, or how stories and knowledge are conveyed in designs, the mother's deep, careful thinking is required to finish her rug. Thinking, then art, make things manifest.[13]

Creativity, thinking, the land, and colors all become conjoined—linked to the primary motif of the book's title "The Colored Land" in the poem, "At Sunset," which once again evokes the cycle of the day and the influence of the sun on earth, how we relate to it, and how we see it. This also has parallels to how the human mind makes associations through language and rhetorical devices such as verse (or song) and linguistic or literary devices such as metaphor and simile:

> The land is white,
> The sun goes down,
> The sky is orange and red
> With streaks of purple.
> The snow looks dyed
> Like wool for a rug. (30)

There are four descriptive lines, one of which suggests causation of the change from snow-covered "white" to its many colors. The last two imaginative lines hinge on a simile: "The snow looks dyed/ Like wool for a rug." Simile, the result of human thought and language use, makes a connection between the sacred, natural, and human worlds, reminding us that there are no divisions, only a world of unity of all parts. Humans were given the gift of weaving and dying wool (M'Closkey 2002, 19), and this matches the ways that Jóhonaa'áí colors the land as he passes over earth each day. And it is the human readers and poets who observe and record this change.

As Ruth K. Brandt mentions in the introduction, the students often made observations about colors and made associations with the various colors of the land. This, of course, is one additional way that the students were sustaining ties with ancestral knowledge that they had gained prior to boarding school and that would persist despite their forced acculturation. Brandt doesn't seem to directly connect their interest with their cultural background as I do, and, indeed, in an earlier resource published for teachers of Indian students, *Seatwork Exercises Based on the F-U-N book, Under the Story Tree, and In Animal Land* (1930), Brandt writes, "Because of Indian children's joy in working with colors at least one of these is a suggested procedure for making a picture based on the story" (1930, 1). The poem "Blue" makes associations with the physical environment/ "this land," animals, with the elements (water, sky), and with items of significance to humans (turquoise beads, sand, blouse):

> Many blues
> In this land,
> Turquoise beads,
> Colored sand.
>
> Mother's blouse,
> Clear blue sky,
> Bluebirds' wings,
> Mountains high.
>
> Water, springs,
> Mesas, too.
> In this land
> So much blue. (13)

Unlike "At Sunset," the speaker of "Blue" recognizes that blue is inherently present in the land ("in this land"), though the appearance of mountains or mesas as blue may be ascribed to the sun's angles, human point of view, or the blue-tinged junipers, piñons, or other evergreens that grow upon them. The blue sky appears because of the status of the sun—that is, depending on the status of cloud cover, time of day, time of the year, and so forth. The listing of all things blue is both a descriptive catalog but also a cultural litany that speaks to cultural relevance and resonance. The color blue, its associations with the precious stone, turquoise, Mt. Taylor/Tsoodził, the South, with the composition of the first hogan, with midday, with planning/nahat'á, and then turquoise's associations with water and sky, all mean that blue is empowering and meaningful. Turquoise plays an important role in creation stories, too, and it is First Woman (in the fourth world), who is given the stone, "which represents the power of speech" (Morris 1997, 7). This association with women and motherhood is strengthened in the reference to "mother's blouse," a constructed item and now "traditional" style that is phrased as shared experience: not "my mother's blouse," not "a mother's blouse," but "mother's blouse." In creation stories, as well, the color blue is associated with the blue beings, including the swallows, whom the insect people encountered (Morris 1997, 5; Zolbrod 1984, 39). Dólii or bluebird is a symbol of peace (Loley 2021, 48), and ceremonies that include sand painting, hatááłii use many colors of sand, including blue. The first two lines and the last two lines stand as bookends, closely paralleling each other: "Many blues/ in this land" and "In this land/ So much blue." This provides a sense of symmetry, of balance that's also matched by the alternating end rhyme scheme of A/B/C/B; D/E/F/E; F/A/B/A. It is a symmetry matched topically by the mention of earth, water, and sky, of mesas, mountains, and springs, of human jewelry and clothing, and of animals and minerals.

One poem, "Beauty," uses the image of a silver necklace and a sand painting to evoke the meaning of the abstract term of the title:

> Beauty moves
> Like a dancer,
> Or water falling.
> But sometimes
> It is still,
> It does not move—
> Like a silver necklace
> Or a sand painting. (Brandt 1937, 56)

In the brief preface to the section "Navajo Games and Dances," the editors write: "One day the children were talking about beauty and trying to say what it was. One child said it meant 'something very, very pretty.' Another said, 'Like beads, silver beads like we have.' Others said, 'a waterfall,' 'a dancer,' 'a sand painting.' Then they made the poem Beauty which tells how some beautiful things moved and some stand still" (51). Through simile and literal examples that are from the natural world, the expressive world of art, from the spiritual and profane, the poem takes us to a profoundly powerful place where the truth comes from the existence of oppositions, that beauty is stillness and movement. In English, the term "beauty" (alternatively, "harmony") is often featured in translations of the word "hózhó," or the ceremony "Hózhóójii," as "Beauty Way," with aspects of a song-prayer translated as "I walk in beauty," or as Laura Tohe writes, "In Beauty it was begun./ In Beauty it continues./ In Beauty,/ In Beauty,/ In Beauty,/ In Beauty" (2021, 130). The complexity of the concept is hardly summed up by this English word, "beauty," something Bojan Louis (Diné) explains in a nonfiction essay on memory, trauma, and writing: "the Diné ideal of hozhó, which can be translated roughly as *the balance of walking and living in harmony, in conjunction with all beings and all things, that each element of the universe has its place and purpose in the* machination *of existence.* Now, *machination* is my word, though I'm fairly certain that it's apt for the translation" (Louis 2021, 303).

One of the elements, among others, that *machinate* the universe is language (the word) itself. For Diné, as with many Indigenous people, language is tied to land and place and is viewed as a gift bestowed on humankind by deities. For this reason, words must be used with care to further strive for and sustain a sense of harmony and balance and not cause harm. Words are understood to have the power to influence the world and shape outcomes. In this way, words have the power to create realities. Several poems in *The Colored Land* reflect on the powerful ways that words and art give rise to realities, producing images in the mind. One poem, "Word Pictures" is a case in point:

> Words are like riders
> On horses fast.
> They make us see pictures
> As they gallop past. (Brandt 1937, 58)

This poem conveys how language captures thought—fleeting, racing, or anxious thoughts, even—and produces images in the mind before instantiating realities. This is parallel to what Sherwin Bitsui said in an interview: "Navajo is thought in motion, a very verb driven language. Everything is tactile, everything is about moving with the world or having the world move within you" (2019, 386). The remarkable painting by Joe Leakity that accompanies this poem features two horses and two riders moving swiftly across the page (see figure 7). In quite literal ways, the process of production went thusly: someone made an observation about language; the concepts were organized formally in verse, collaboratively; the poems were shared with older students in Santa Fe; and this image was produced (bringing the concept into reality). Now, readers across time are using both components to continue to see and understand this reality in each of our respective minds. The student poets note that it is the riders, not the horses, that are words, and the idea of language is produced by humans and their cultures to transcend physical limitations and different dimensions.

WORDS ARE LIKE RIDERS

Joe Leakity

FIGURE 7. "Words Are Like Riders" from *The Colored Land.*

Another poem, "My Picture," by the Tohatchi students similarly meditates on a drawing and the authorial and artistic power to bring a reality into existence:

I made a picture of a horse—
A running horse,
A bucking horse.
I made a cowboy riding him.
I named the cowboy "Slim." (Brandt 1937, 66)

This simple, descriptive poem—an "occasional poem"—is similar to other poems in meter and similar in the use of appositive, adjectival clauses ("a running horse" and "a bucking horse"), all of which suggest that the teachers may be modeling or providing structures to plug original thought into. Two of the lines modify the first, and two of the verbs emphasize creativity: "made" used with the first-person pronoun, as does the phrase "I named," which also emphasizes the power to define and bestow a name upon others, suggesting that artistic creativity extends a sense of autonomy and authority.[14] The poem is accompanied by an accomplished drawing of a bucking horse, beautifully arched, with a cowboy seated upon its back (see figure 8).

I NAMED THE COWBOY "SLIM"

FIGURE 8. "I Named the Cowboy 'Slim'" from *The Colored Land*.

The drawing is ascribed to a student from Santa Fe, Joe Vigil. While Vigil's portrait is dynamic and artful, its presence and attribution create some dissonance with the content of the poem itself being produced by students in Tohatchi. The image is an imagined version of the horse and cowboy drawn by students in Tohatchi who found occasion to write a poem about their own drawing.

"Unity" and "If" are two other poems featuring horses that deserve attention. As the editor points out in a section introduction on "Navajo Children and Animals," students have an interest in and affection for animals, including goats, sheep, donkeys, horses, and chickens (Brandt 1937, 43). These prose sections and poems emphasize a sense of kinship and interdependence, emphasizing K'é, of the relationality to all living beings, a complex term that Lloyd Lee has described as the "integral system designed to understand the relationship that Diné peoples have to one another and all living things on Earth and in the universe" (2014, 182). Like "Word Poems," "Unity" emphasizes movement and oneness in the midst of movement:

First
I'm on my horse,
We move,
Galloping, galloping
Together we move,
Now
I'm part of my horse. (Brandt 1937, 50)

The union is not instant. In fact, we're reminded that this relationship emerges over time, as signaled by chronological markers "First" and "Now." The second line employs first person, but the central three lines emphasize collectivity through the plural personal pronoun, "We" and "we," both conjoined with the verb "move." Eventually, "now," the speaker is "part of my horse," reminding us of the unity that exists in the midst of separation (my horse). Without a drawing to accompany this poem, readers are left to ponder where this duo is moving, where they are galloping to; the field of the page, primarily white space, leads readers to envision the two moving together across the land. The poem issues a subtle and powerful statement of resistance to individuation and individualism, emphasizing instead mutuality. Irvin Morris's (Diné) autobiographical sections of *From the Glittering World* emphasize a similar oneness. For Morris, this is particularly apparent in the chapter, "Shilíí" (My horse). Morris first describes in sensuous detail his ascent in the mountains, his horse Ace's assuredness and even footing, and the rightness with the world while riding Ace in this place: "I can disappear into the forest and emerge somewhere else, someplace where I can believe it is a hundred years ago or even further back . . . The forest is timeless . . . There, in the absolute stillness, I can believe there is no Kit Carson. No Niña, Pinta, or Santa Maria" (1997, 135). Here, one might argue, he feels unaffected by the forces of settler and extractive colonialism and the legacies of empire. Morris belongs and is home, finding shelter and meaning. Indigenous scholar and theorist Glen Coulthard (Yellowknife Dene) articulates how this sense of belonging on land lays the foundation for rebellion: "Place is a way of knowing, experiencing, and relating with the world—and these ways of knowing often guide forms of resistance to power relations that threaten to erase or destroy our senses of place" (2010, 79–80). A sense of unity and of kinship with other beings in place guide a sense of resistance and rejection of imposed systems of knowledge, of values/priorities, and institutional power to control.

While "Unity" might argue that this and many of the other previous poems discussed make powerful claims against Western acculturation by valuing Diné family, culture, and place, "If" operates from a place where alternative realities, if not futures, are imagined:

If I were a pony,
A spotted pinto pony,
A good racing pony,
I would run away from school.
I'd gallop on the mesa
And I'd eat on the mesa,
And I'd sleep on the mesa,
And I'd never think of school. (Brandt 1937, 44)

This poem deepens the mutuality and interdependence of the poem "Unity" and imagines the freedom that would be possible if one were simply not a human child, a student forced to be at school. The title and first word, a word that cues the subjunctive mode in English, issues this conjecture, a *what if*, an alternative possibility—life fully lived on the open mesa, not within the strictures of school—eating, sleeping, galloping. "Would" in the poem's fourth line, its middle line, provides the first response, repeating in contraction in the next four lines: "I'd." "Would" is a modal auxiliary verb, and here it also expresses conditionality and desire.

The eight lines have roughly even syllable count—6/7/6/6/7/7/7/7— which creates a formal syncopation that mimics galloping. This poem metaphorically imagines another world being "away from school," in a world where "I'd never think of school." The parallelism of the fourth line and the last line emphasizes this point: "I would run away from school . . . / And I'd never think of school." According to the introduction by Brandt, this poem began as a collaboration after one boy named Chee, who, seeing a horse running on the mesa, "sighed, 'I wish I could be that pony!'" (1937, 7). Brandt's comments seem to ignore the critique altogether and ascribe it to a child's daydreaming. In fact, the image found on page 44 by Elias Montoya serves as the cover image of the book; a great deal of irony abounds in terms of the desires attached to this renegade pony emblematizing a book about Diné students' experiences at boarding school (see figure 9). The simple drawing on its own offers no context about boarding schools. Here, the poetry and the implicit meanings of its lines deepen the import of the image.

Elsewhere in the book, in the sections on Navajo girls and Navajo boys, the students describe a fictional child in each. Regarding the girl: "Nah-bah goes to school. The school is near her home" (27). This is descriptive and withholds qualification. By contrast, the section on the boy says, "Navajo Boy goes to school. He likes to go to school" (28), a comment that sits in stark opposition to the poetic voice that speaks volumes across the decades.[15] Imagining a life free of the strictures of boarding school ("And, I'd never think of school") does issue a critique of the institution, but one that is general. Read in the context of these other writings about the richness of life outside of school,

I'D GALLOP ON THE MESA

FIGURE 9. "I'd Gallop on the Mesa" from *The Colored Land*.

it is easy to see that the poem indicts a system that cuts students off from this wellspring of knowledge.

The last two poems to which I turn heighten this critique of Western epistemologies and Western systems of knowledge, and, at the very least, express some ambiguity and ambivalence about them. The titular poem, "The Colored Land," was composed, according to the foreword, by a group of girls—referred to as girl scouts—who had returned from an outing to the mountains. Given the content of other poems in the collection, as previously discussed, it is not surprising that this poem provides the title for the whole as it coalesces the multiple ways that this book positions the experiences and cultural knowledge of Diné students as rooted in this land, in the ways that Dudley Patterson (a Cibecue horseman) famously said:

> Wisdom sits in places . . . You must remember everything about them. You must learn their names. You must remember what happened at them long ago. You must think about it and keep on thinking about it. Then your mind will become smoother and smoother. (Basso 1995, 127)

Indigenous wisdom, particularly within Western institutions is always under threat. This is especially true in boarding schools, where, as Mishuana Goeman (Tonawanda Band of Seneca) reminds us, the focus was ultimately on "the colonial making of place and an alienation of the body from land as a life blood . . . They were deeply concerned with disciplining bodies, distancing Indigenous people from land, and destroying the cultural ways that nurtured relationship to land and their communities" (2015, 81).

This clash of epistemologies is most definitely represented in "The Colored Land." Instead of highlighting the loss of Indigenous ways of knowing, this poem suggests that the students are ready to challenge Western paradigms, despite the institution's intentions. Upon returning from their outing, one girl wondered where the colors of the sunset went when the sun faded. Her answer to her own question was, "I think it goes down into the earth—way down. We could see it in the air, but it is just fire way down in the earth—and hot. Maybe—but I think the color goes there" (Brandt 1937, 7). While this poem offers a hypothesis of what happens, it also offers a reminder that the poem's speaker has been keeping track of what's been proffered as "the truth" by educators. This reminds me of what Linda Tuhiwai Smith (Māori) so powerfully shares: that Indigenous Peoples' knowledge of their colonizers is part of Indigenous knowledge (Smith 1999, 45). Knowledge—or facts, or theories—is delightfully reduced to "this thing" in the words of the speaker of "The Colored Land":

> I heard this thing—
> In the center of the earth it is hot.
> Maybe you believe it—maybe not.
>
> I think this thing—
> All is color
> In the center of the world,
> Red—purple—blue—
> Orange—yellow—gold.
> I think this thing.
>
> It came from the sunsets
> When day grew old,
> Came from the sunsets
> When day grew cold.
> I think this thing. (Brandt 1937, 16)

Scientific information from textbooks about the earth's core is characterized as "this thing" and is something that some believe to be true, while others may not.[16] Set alongside "this thing" is another "thing" thought by the poet/the poem's speaker: the many-colored center of the world comes from the sun setting each day. The hypothesis is stated in the second stanza and theorized in the third. The poem's structure is thesis, antithesis, and if not synthesis, then interpretation and claim. The last line "I think this thing" is repeated three times and envelopes the middle stanza, concluding the poem. These lines sit in contrast, if not rebuttal, to the first line, "I heard this thing." While the poem is playful and exploratory, given the context in which it is written, it evidences ambivalence about received knowledge that might be rejected by alternative paradigms and epistemologies. Knowledge from instruction is reduced in status or equal to independent thought: "I heard this thing" = "I think this thing." As discussed earlier, regarding the sun and its role within Diné culture, the student here is finding a way to integrate cultural knowledge as part of the explanation for how the heat from the sun that journeys through the sky, and rests at night, is retained.

"My Thinking," the very last poem in the book, the proverbial last word, heightens the refusal present in the poem "The Colored Land." Indeed, I've borrowed a line from this poem for the title of the article because it profoundly asserts a sovereignty of intellect and a willingness to let ways of knowing (and thus, thinking) to be unreconcilable and perhaps even unfathomable:

> If I do not believe you
> The things you say,
> Maybe I will not tell you.
> That is my way.
>
> Maybe you think I believe you
> That thing you say,
> But always my thoughts stay with me
> My own way. (80)

While the student poet makes no claim to a particular Diné way of thinking, given the context in which the work is presented, this interpretation is hard to resist especially given that the poems were crafted collaboratively. There's an acknowledgment that a unique way of thinking will persist. In speaking about the uniqueness and "landed-ness" of Indigenous epistemologies that continue through generations, Dian Million (Tanana Athabascan) acknowledges that while there are/may have been shifts in expression or form due to contingencies of experiences under colonialism, "The legatees of non-Western, place-based epistemologies collectively perform their knowledge and beliefs, variably transmitted through their prior generations. These generations continue to dream, dance, sing, and practice our knowledge and experiences into new meaning" (Million 2015, 339). "My Thinking" is empowering and hopeful, and in this way reminds me of Simon Ortiz's (Acoma) beautiful poem, "Enormous Knowledge":

It is amazing
how much knowledge
we have of hope.

Whisper bravely
into the dark,
Heart,
whisper bravely. (Ortiz 1994, 39)

Ortiz's poem emphasizes the hope that we must retain in our movement forward, toward an unknown future. Were the anonymous students at the Tohatchi Boarding School using poetic words as whispers into the darkness? Could they ever have imagined that one day in the future there would be readers spending time with their poems, that the poems would speak to the generations that followed? In her letter to readers at the outset of *The Diné Reader,* Esther Belin characterizes the contents of her edited anthology as "a time capsule gently crafted together. They are a roadmap, documenting and redefining home" (2021, 3). And that includes a book such as *The Colored Land,* perhaps one of the first to record in English the creative, poetic expression oriented toward a broad audience. It serves as a time capsule and roadmap, documenting and providing direction.

These last two poems—"The Colored Land" and "My Thinking"—exemplify some profound ambivalence about different ways of knowing, paradigm clashes, potential epistemological divides, offering readers some insights into a complexity at play. The poems and much of the art in *The Colored Land* can be considered acts of intellectual and creative sovereignty, what Anishinaabe writer and theorist Gerald Vizenor refers to as survivance: "an active sense of presence, the continuance of native stories, not a mere reaction, or a survivable name . . . [the] renunciations of dominance, tragedy and victimry" (vii). The students' output represents an important celebration of the power of family, of a relational connection to land and place—all qualities of Diné ways of knowing and being. In this way, the poems issue a refusal of the epistemic violence to which the students are being subjected. Despite the indoctrination they are experiencing at boarding school, the students are theorizing ways forward. Ultimately, it is the culturally rich and tacit messages of the poetry and art and stories that build bridges to Diné futures. The student writers from Tohatchi and the student artists from Santa Fe are not only remembering the return to the past and the ways of their forebearers, but also finding ways, even in their constrained present lives, to take possession of this knowledge. They forge a path forward that is continuous with the past and that connects them to home and to the knowledge that originates from and is resonant in the many colors of Diné Bikéyah.

JEFF BERGLUND is a professor of English at Northern Arizona University which sits at the base of the San Francisco Peaks, in Flagstaff, Arizona, on homelands sacred to Indigenous Peoples throughout the region who have lived here for millennia and who will forever call this place home. Berglund's research and teaching focuses on Native American literature, comparative Indigenous film, and U.S. multiethnic literature. His books include *Cannibal Fictions: American Explorations of Colonialism, Race, Gender, and Sexuality* (2006), *Sherman Alexie: A Collection of Critical Essays* (co-editor, 2010), *Indigenous Pop: Native American Music from Jazz to Hip Hop* (co-editor, 2016), *The Diné Reader: An Anthology of Navajo Literature* (co-editor, 2021), and *Indigenous Peoples Rise Up: The Global Ascendancy of Social Media Activism* (co-editor, 2021).

References

Aronolith, Wilson Jr. 1992. *Foundation of Navajo Culture.* Self-published: printed in Navajoland.

Basso, Keith H. 1996. *Wisdom Sits in Places.* Albuquerque: University of New Mexico Press.

Belin, Esther G., Jeff Berglund, Connie J. Jacobs, and Anthony K. Webster, eds. 2021. *The Diné Reader: An Anthology of Navajo Literature.* Tucson: University of Arizona Press.

———. 1999. *From the Belly of My Beauty.* Tucson: University of Arizona Press.

———. 2019. "Poem Making as Making Space." In *Native Voices: Indigenous American Poetry, Craft, and Conversations,* edited by CMarie Fuhrman and Dean Rader, 343–45. North Adams: Tupelo.

Begay, Manley A. Jr. 2017. "The Path of Navajo Sovereignty in Traditional Education: Harmony, Disruption, Distress, and Restoration of Harmony." In *Navajo Sovereignty: Understandings and Visions of the Diné People,* edited by Lloyd Lee, 57–90. Tucson: University of Arizona Press.

Benes, Rebecca C. 2004. *Native American Picture Books of Change: The Art of Historic Children's Editions.* Santa Fe: Museum of New Mexico Press.

Bitsui, Sherwin. 2019. "The Motion of Poetic Landscape: An Interview with Sherwin Bitsui." In *Native Voices: Indigenous American Poetry, Craft, and Conversations,* edited by CMarie Fuhrman and Dean Rader, 386–87. North Adams: Tupelo.

Brandt, Ruth K., ed. 1937. *The Colored Land: A Navajo Indian Book Written and Illustrated by Navajo Children.* New York: Charles Scribner's Sons.

———. 1930. *Seatwork Exercises Based on the F-U-N book, Under the Story Tree, and In Animal Land.* Washington, D.C.: Department of the Interior, Office of Indian Affairs.

———. 1935. "We Make Our Own Books." *Indians at Work* 2, no. 21 (June 15): 25–27.

Collier, John, ed. 1936. Special Children's Number by Indian Children: Indians at Work. Washington, D.C.: Office of Indian Affairs.

Coulthard, Glen. 2010. "Place Against Empire: Understanding Indigenous Anti-Colonialism." *Affinities: A Journal of Radical Theory, Culture, and Action* 4, no. 2: 79–83.

Denetdale, Jennifer Nez. 2007. *Reclaiming Diné History: The Legacies of Navajo Chief Manuelito and Juanita.* Tucson: University of Arizona Press.

Donovan, Bill. 2018. "50 Years Ago: Ft. Defiance Played a Role in Diné History." *The Navajo Times* May 24. Navajotimes.com.

Faris, James C. 2004. *Navajo and Photography: A Critical History of an American People.* Salt Lake City: University of Utah Press.

Greyeyes, Wendy. 2022. *A History of Navajo Nation Education: Disentangling Our Sovereign Body.* Tucson: University of Arizona Press.

Goeman, Mishuana. 2015. "Land as Life: Unsettling the Logics of Containment." In *Native Studies Keywords,* edited by Stephanie Nohelani Teves, Andrea Smith, and Michelle H. Raheja. 71–89. Tucson: University of Arizona Press.

Emery, Jacqueline. 2017. *Recovering Native American Writings in the Boarding School Press.* Edited by Jacqueline Emery. Lincoln: University of Nebraska Press.

Hyer, Sally. 1990. *One House, One Voice, One Heart: Native American Education at the Santa Fe Indian School.* Santa Fe: Museum of New Mexico Press.

Katanski, Amelia V. 2005. *Learning to Write "Indian": The Boarding-school Experience and American Indian Literature.* Norman: University of Oklahoma Press.

King, Farina. 2018. *Earth Memory Compass: Diné Landscapes and Education in the Twentieth Century.* Lawrence: University of Kansas Press.

King, Farina, Michael P. Taylor, and James R. Swensen. *Returning Home:* Diné *Creative Works from the Intermountain Indian School.* Tucson: University of Arizona Press, 2021.

Krupat, Arnold. 2021. *Boarding School Voices: Carlisle Indian School Students Speak.* Lincoln: University of Nebraska Press.

———. 2018. *Changed Forever: American Indian Boarding-School Literature. Vol I.* Albany: State University of New York Press.

———. 2020. *Changed Forever: American Indian Boarding-School Literature.* Vol. II. Albany: State University of New York Press.

Lee, Lloyd L. 2014. *Diné Perspectives: Revitalizing and Reclaiming Navajo Thought,* edited by Lloyd L. Lee. Tucson: University of Arizona Press.

Loley, Manny. 2021. "Hodeeyáádą́ą́' Dólii Hataał Jiní (When We Emerged, Bluebird Was Singing, They Say)." *Pleiades: Literature in Context* 41, no. 2: 48–53. http://doi.org/10.1353/plc.2021.0033.

Lomawaima, K. Tsianina. 1995. *They Called It Prairie Light: The Story of Chilocco Indian School.* Lincoln: University of Nebraska Press.

Lomawaima, K. Tsianina and Teresa. L. McCarty. 2006. *"To Remain an Indian": Lessons in Democracy from a Century of Native American Education.* New York: Teachers College Press.

Louis, Bojan. 2021. "Nizhoní dóó 'a'ani' dóó até'él'í dóó ayoo'o'oni (Beauty & Memory & Abuse & Love)." In *The Diné Reader: An Anthology of Navajo Literature,* edited by Esther G. Belin, Jeff Berglund, Connie J. Jacobs, and Anthony K. Webster. 302–8. Tucson: University of Arizona Press.

Lowe, Blackhorse, dir. 2013. "Shimásání." 2009; Másáni LLC. Killer Whale PR+M https://projektor.com/watch/1003.

M'Closkey, Kathy. 2002. *Swept Under the Rug: A Hidden History of Navajo Weaving.* Albuquerque: University of New Mexico Press.

Million, Dian. 2015. "Epistemology." In *Native Studies Keywords,* edited by Stephanie Nohelani Teves, Andrea Smith, and Michelle H. Raheja. 339—46. Tucson: University of Arizona Press.

Morris, Irvin. 1997. *From the Glittering World: A Navajo Story.* Norman: University of Oklahoma Press.

NAVAJOCODE. 2018. "Navajo Hair Bun." November 7. https://navajocodetalkers .org/navajo-hair-bun/.

Ortiz, Simon. 1994. *After and Before Lightning.* Tucson: University of Arizona Press.

Roessel, Ruth., and Broderick H. Johnson. 1974. *Navajo Livestock Reduction: A National Disgrace.* 1st ed. Chinle, Arizona: Navajo Community College Press.

Roessel, Ruth. 1981. *Women in Navajo Society.* Rough Rock, Arizona: Rough Rock Demonstration School.

Skeets, Jake. 2020. "The Memory Field: Musings on the Diné Perspective of Time, Memory, and Land." *Emergence Magazine,* October 14. https://emergence magazine.org/essay/the-memory-field/

Schwarz, Maureen Trudelle. 1997. "Unraveling the Anchoring Cord: Navajo Relocation, 1974 to 1996." *American Anthropologist* 99, no. : 43—55. https:// doi.org/10.1525/aa.1997.99.1.43.

Smith, Linda Tuhiwai. 1999. *Decolonizing Methodologies: Research and Indigenous Peoples.* London: Zed Books.

Tohe, Laura. 1999. *No Parole Today.* Albuquerque, NM: West End Press.

———. 2021. "Within Dinétah, Our People's Spirits Remain Strong." In *The Diné Reader: An Anthology of Navajo Literature,* edited by Esther G. Belin, Jeff Berglund, Connie J. Jacobs, and Anthony K. Webster. 126—30. Tucson: University of Arizona Press.

Thompson, Kerry Francis. 2009. "*Ałkidáá 'Da Hooghanée (They Used To Live Here): An Archaeological Study Of Late Nineteenth And Early Twentieth Century Navajo Hogan Households And Federal Indian Policy.*" PhD diss., University of Arizona.

Vizenor, Gerald Robert. 1999. *Manifest Manners: Narratives of Postindian Survivance.* University of Nebraska Press.

Woody, Elizabeth. 2021. Interview. In *The Diné Reader: An Anthology of Navajo Literature,* edited by Esther G. Belin, Jeff Berglund, Connie J. Jacobs, and Anthony K. Webster. 106—8. Tucson: University of Arizona Press.

Yazzie, Cora Ben Gould. 1935. "Wedding." *Indians at Work* 2, no. 21 (June 15): 23—24.

Zolbrod, Paul. 1987. Diné Bahane': The Navajo Creation Story. Albuquerque: University of New Mexico Press.

Notes

1. I'm grateful to Anthony K. Webster for first bringing it to our collective attention. I was impressed by transcriptions of two of the poems that he shared but was deeply captivated by the full book when I finally saw it in its entirety.

2. Brandt 1937, 53. Besides "hogan," one other word is offered in a footnote as a preferred substitution for a disparaging term: "Sq— is the white man's name for an Indian woman. The Navajo name, N'dá-a, sounds much better."

3. See Katanski 2005, Emery 2017, and Krupat 2018, 2020, and 2021, among others.

4. King cites the work of K. Tsianina Lomawaima and Teresa L. McCarty's discussion of so-called safety zones through which the federal policymakers allowed for cultural expression, while all the same prioritizing assimilation, acculturation, and "Americanization." See Lomawaima and McCarty 2006, 5.

5. Benes's book discusses later projects in this vein that also involved Ann Clark and that enlisted other Diné artists such as Andrew Tsinajinnie and Gerald Nailor (2004, 73–80).

6. The tsiiyééł is a hair bun worn by men and women, today tied in white yarn, that represents clear thinking; its making is both a cultural and a spiritual practice, connecting humans to first man and first woman whose hair was made by rainclouds, and the string, used to wrap it, made by the sun. One who wears the tsiiyééł has gathered their thoughts and is focused (Aronolith 1992, 176; Roessel 1981, 80; and NAVAJOCODE 2010).

7. With an introduction by John Collier, Commissioner of Indian Affairs, the special issue featured fifty-one pages of work from Indigenous students who were identified as Navajo, Zuni, Jemez, Acoma, Taos, Santa Ana, Santo Domingo, Pima, Shoshone, Chippewa, Sioux (from Standing Rock, Rosebud, Pine Ridge, and Fort Totten), Blackfeet, and Mescalero Apache. Other students were identified by boarding schools rather than tribal nations: Riverside Boarding School, Goshute Day School, Metlakatla School, Sequoyah School, Shoshone School, Santa Fe School, and Heart Butte Day School, among others. Of note, fifteen other Navajo student writers in this special issue were identified by name, including Cora Ben Gould Yazzie whose work "Wedding" had been included in a 1935 issue of Indians at Work. Besides Tohatchi, Shiprock, and Crownpoint, these Navajo students attended Leupp School, Southern Navajo Boarding School, Chin Le [sic] Day School, Toadlena Indian School, Western Navajo School.

8. To minimize confusion in my analysis, I default to the singular "speaker" or "poet" when discussing poetry—if for no other reason than to parallel the singular "I" that appears in the poems. It should also be noted that there is no single correct way to authenticate that the publication includes poetry that was exclusively written and shaped by the students themselves. It is tempting to wonder about this, but the vocabulary, the content, and the syntax, in particular, lead me to trust that they're largely, if not exclusively, the work of students at Tohatchi and not Brandt nor the students' teacher. This is not the case for the form of the book and the placement of its various components, including the solicitation of artwork from students at the Santa Fe Indian School.

9. It's tempting to also consider other factors that deepen Diné individuals' sense of home, further solidified by the burial of umbilical cords (see Schwarz 1997, 43).

10. Irving Berlin's 1918 lyrics were later revised to the more familiar version published in 1938. Present-day readers might find it interesting that the line, "This is the land for me," anticipates Woody Guthrie's 1944 ballad, published seven years after the publication of *The Colored Land*.

11. This section on the students constructing hogans in their classroom at the school in Chinle further disrupts the claimed authenticity as laid out in the introduction: that the written work was the product of students at the Tohatchi Boarding School.

12. In Tohe's story, "So I Blow Smoke in Her Face," in contrast to "Night at Home," the narrator's memory of home emboldens her to rebel against the dormitory matron that leads to her expulsion and eventual return home (Tohe 1999).

13. This emphasis on women's labor regarding weaving contrasts with what Diné historian Jennifer Nez Denetdale suggests was the norm during this period and the ways that most stereotypical images of Navajo women and rugs obscured this connection (Denetdale 2007, 93).

14. Inversely, this recalls Laura Tohe's poem, "The Names," from *No Parole Today,* where she references the boarding school experience of not having control of how one is known and how one's names are pronounced.

15. The ending of Blackhorse Lowe's (Diné) powerful short film, "Shimásání" (2009), set in 1934, considers the plight of two Diné sisters, one at boarding school, one who yearns to join her. It probes the emotional and familial landscape of the seismic changes that would indelibly disrupt Diné lifeways.

16. Indeed, it was in the mid-1920s (Harold Jeffreys) and mid-1930s (Inge Lehmann) that new European discoveries were still being made about the molten and solid cores of the earth, even though such has been proposed, though not proven, as far back as 1692 (Edmund Haley).

KURTIS BOYER *and* CHRIS ANDERSEN

Defining a Nation: Métis Nation Building in the Face of Epistemic Injustice

Abstract

Over the past four decades, Indigenous political claims "in" Canada have come increasingly to assume a nationalist form. Efforts at instilling a national identity play an abundantly clear role in Indigenous nation (re)building: they hold the potential to concretize internal solidarity, mobilize community to pursue long-term goals, and they aid in overcoming a host of collective action problems. However, for national claims to play such a role, it is necessary that outside groups recognize a community's national identity and accept it as distinct. That is to say, nationhood must be thought about in terms of its occurrence in an (unequally) relational context: claims to a national distinction occur in competition with other claims, in a field of struggle and competition in which actors possess varying abilities to enforce/support claims and to have those claims recognized by others. In this regard, the concept of *epistemic injustice* is especially useful to engage with the differential capacity of communities to claim and enforce national claims unto others. Our analysis, which focuses specifically on the case of the Métis, pays particular attention to the widespread misrecognitions that occur when a dominant social group marginalizes Métis claims to nationhood. Through this exploration, our article contributes to a better understanding of relational conditions overall and the ways in which identity and nationhood can support the process of Indigenous nation building.

IN NAVIGATING THE TURBULENT WATERS of colonial history, Indigenous Peoples have been compelled to confront and adapt to numerous external pressures threatening their very existence. Central to this struggle has been the relentless challenge of preserving and asserting their distinct cultural identities in the face of policies aimed at assimilation and cultural erasure. Nationhood, including cultural understandings, rules of conduct, and kinship in particular, are emphasized as key markers that have helped Indigenous Peoples survive colonization and its accompanying assimilation policies to maintain, as Cornell states, "the binding sinews of a shared consciousness and identity."[1]

Often overlooked, however, is the fact that Indigenous national identities are always/already expressed in a *relational* context that plays a constitutively powerful role in governance and in the possibility for political agency. In other words, Indigenous nationhood and its *claims* for recognition are largely dependent on whether others (including other Indigenous nations[2] as well as non-Indigenous people in Canada) accept that identity as distinct. As we explore in this essay, ensuring that others see and recognize your nationhood requires the epistemic authority necessary to enforce the meaning and value of one's national identity as well as its distinctiveness in relation to the broader society. Nation building is, in short, a fundamentally claims-*based* and claims-*making* process.[3]

For Métis political actors—especially, perhaps, relative to other Indigenous political actors in Canada—the pursuit of self-government has long been challenged by a broader epistemic environment. Boyer and Simard characterize this environment as a narrower (read: deficient) conceptual "bandwidth" within which the Canadian public is often unable to situate Métis claims to Indigenous nationhood.[4] Indeed, within this epistemic environment, certain non-Métis have mobilized the notion of collective deficiency to deny the existence of a distinct national Métis identity. For the Métis, being a postcontact Indigenous people[5] in a nation-state such as Canada, which is so deeply wedded to understanding Indigeneity as a precontact phenomena, has severely complicated (if not outright strangled) the Métis' ability to be recognized as culturally distinctive, let alone "fully Indigenous."[6] The Métis people's distinctive relationships to and experiences with colonial projects of the British—and more recently, the Canadian—state (some of which are discussed in this article), leave the Métis particularly vulnerable to the selective appropriation or complete denial of what it means to be Métis.[7] In a relational context where national identities other than those claimed and reproduced by the colonial state are commonly misunderstood or outright denied, the nation (re)building process for the Métis people—the claims they make and, indeed, are allowed to make—are acutely vulnerable to arguments that fundamentally question the moral and practical possibility of Métis self-government and the "differential citizenship" it entails.[8]

Scrutinizing the interplay between Métis nationhood and the epistemic context shaped by external (mis)recognition, we posit that the historical colonial backdrop in Canada significantly constrains the Métis community's capacity to assert and delineate their nationhood's essence and value to non-Indigenous actors. This analysis aims to unpack the complexities surrounding the acknowledgment, interpretation, or negation of Métis national claims within contemporary discourses, thereby contributing to a better understanding of the factors influencing Métis sovereignty assertions. We begin by differentiating between nations and nation-states—discussing their necessary but sometimes uneasy, fricative relationship—in the context of positioning national*ism* as fundamentally a *claims-making process.*[9] From there, we proceed to trace the origins of the current epistemic environment within which nationalist Métis claims to Indigeneity are situated. Providing several stark historical examples that have shaped this landscape, we unpack how "ethnoracial struggles of the past"[10] have winnowed the discursive and narrative space within which Métis national claims—and attendant nation building by its proponents—can take place today. We begin, however, with a conceptual discussion of nationalism since Indigenous nationalisms and their "fit" with respect to colonial states' national claims have co-constitutively shaped not only Canada's claims to nationhood but those of the Métis as well.

Nations, States, and Nation-States: From Things to Claims

In the broad span of the scholarly literature on nations and nationalism, "nations" are often positioned as "substantialist containers"[11] that possess a sum of a nation's collective cultural and political markers, anchored in common roots and territory. "Nationalism" is likewise positioned in terms of the various symbols, institutions, discourses, traditional practices, and mythologies to which any given "nation-ness" is anchored.[12] Doyens of the nationalism literature have pinned these positionings of nation and nationalism to modernity and the industrial processes of northern Europe that characterized them (with varying degrees of disagreement regarding the extent to which "pre-national" cultural collectivities are key actors in subsequent nationalist political reorganizations).[13] In any case—and particularly relevant here for reasons we will elaborate below—such arguments indelibly link the growth and unfolding of nations (as either a product of or a co-constitutive element) to the growth of liberal *states.* This is partly why the phrase "nation-state" seems to roll off the tongues of most students of nations, states, and nation-states so easily.

Of course, the concept of the "modern state" possesses its own scholarly pedigree separate from that of nationhood and nationalism. As most students of modern states are aware, the idea of a state as a centralized political and legal "power container"[14] has existed prior to the formation of *nation*-states.[15] According to French historian Ferdinand Braudel, for example, the modern state possess(ed) three central elements that anchored "its" stability as a form of administrative power: an ability to "secure obedience" in its legitimacy while maintaining a monopoly on the use of legitimate force (also central to German sociologist Max Weber's classic definition);[16] the exertion of control over economic life "near and far" to ensure, among other things, the orderly circulation of goods and sufficient monies through the collection of taxes to fund its own expenditures (administration, wars, etc.); and the power to direct spiritual/religious life in ways that strengthened its legitimacy. In short, the modern state came to exert an increasingly powerful administrative role in the everyday lives of those it accepted as its citizens.

Braudel's definition is useful for highlighting the extent to which the powers of the modern state rely upon their administrative "reach." For our purposes here, even more significant than his positioning of certain "tasks" as central to modern state formation and maintenance is his emphasis that, rather than constituting natural entities, states—and the edicts and policies that characterized them—were/are administratively *directed*. This insight is crucial because to understand state actors as direct*ors* necessarily means that we must also understand nations in general—and Indigenous nations in particular—as existing in ongoing resonance/friction of/with (often state-directed) logics, programs and policies.[17] This positioning is somewhat at odds with populist depictions of nations as the natural, organic outcome of a group of people who share common ethnic, linguistic, or religious roots and, as such, common beliefs and values. Nonetheless, the process of turning states into nation-states is also the partial effect of logics, programs, and policies of state actors that powerfully shape what nation-states come to look like in any geopolitical context and of "minority nationalist" projects to account for those practices.

In their famous declaration, historians Hobsbawm and Ranger stated that nations not only rely upon, but, in a very real way, are based (at least in part) on "invented traditions."[18] Their point in making this claim was to suggest that certain traditions otherwise commonly understood as venerable, and even ancient, were instead of a more (sometimes far more) recent vintage and that their legitimacy and presumed links to a distant past were produced and cemented in popular culture through their repeated use (which, in itself, links us not just to a past but to a *selected* past). These uses were often part of or in response to state-sponsored projects. In their classic sociological discussion of the modern state—a discussion that arguably refracted a broader discussion on the ability of state-based power to shape culture and our everyday subjectivities—Corrigan and Sayer likewise suggest that much of the power of the contemporary (nation-)state lies in its ability to make authoritative pronouncements and have these (largely) followed by broad substrates of the public.[19] In their elegant phrasing—a quote that has been used widely in modern state formation literature—they write that "states state . . . they define in great detail acceptable forms and images of social activity and individual and collective identity; they regulate, in empirically specifiable ways, much—very much, by the twentieth century—of social life."[20] In sum, states—and nation-states in particular—play a powerful role in shaping the kinds of nationalist claims that can be made within their territorial ambit.

Thus, to understand nationalism not just as a theory but as both a political and a cultural *claim* to legitimacy and unity (a "system of cultural representation," to use cultural theorist Stuart Hall's familiar phrasing), it becomes important to ask the question of how nation-states attempt to incorporate collectivities that existed prior to the growth and effective control exerted by state authority. Hall encourages us to understand nationalism and nation-ness precisely in terms of the fricative, juxtapositional, or sometimes even defiantly oppositional claims to nation that characterize the internal cultural and political lives of many nation-states around the world.[21] For Hall, nations—or in our terms, their adherents' claims to nationalist solidarity—always (and only) exist in the midst of two oppositional forces: one centripetal, the other centrifugal.[22] *Centrifugal* forces are those rooted in cultural differences (in their variegated forms) that, Hall argues, labor more or less effectively according to their less dominant positions within the nation-state to undercut the otherwise unifying claims of dominant political and cultural sects of the nation-state, including its authorized actors and the cultural projects they champion (what Brubaker has elsewhere termed the "nationalized state"[23]). The analytical sum of this position is that "the seemingly natural discursive linking of "nation" with "state" (that is, "one nation = one state") is belied by the physical and symbolic violence [often required to anchor] its legitimacy."[24]

National identity appears central to many (though crucially, not all) contemporary Indigenous modes of collective understanding and solidarity making, just as it is for non-Indigenous forms.[25] Indeed, Indigenous collectivities' perception and presentation of ourselves and our histories in terms of "nation-ness" has proven to be a key element of our pursuits of self-governance. As noted earlier, national identity provides a collective toolbox of symbols, narratives and stories that attempt to unite people, a necessary requirement for the pursuit of collective goals such as more or less autonomous self-rule within a liberal nation-state like Canada, while pushing back against alternative attempts at categorization (such as, in the context of the Métis, racial categorization).

Narratives of Indigenous nationhood not only emphasize a shared place to which individuals feel allegiance but also highlight what distinguishes their claims from non-Indigenous claims to nationhood. Collective narratives that speak to a distinction based on original *and prior* shared relationships to land and territory provide an important moral and political ground for self-determination. Such claims are not always (or even mostly) secessionist.[26] Indigenous claims to nationhood—including, we would argue, those of the Métis Nation—exist conceptually within a model of political power based on the idea of *nested* claims of sovereignty. As deployed by Mohawk scholar Audra Simpson, this phrase is itself rooted in the idea that competing ideas of sovereignty can and do exist, often in tension with one another. In colonial contexts in particular, Indigenous claims to sovereignty belie the otherwise totalizing claims of the colonial state and, in Simpson's elegant phrasing, demonstrate in both theory and practice that settler state claims to cultural and political legitimacy do not constitute the only "political show in town . . . Like Indigenous bodies, Indigenous sovereignties and Indigenous political orders prevail within and apart from settler governance."[27]

For Indigenous peoples, nationalist claims[28]—their expressions and the determinants of their recognition—are thus often, by necessity, related to the specific sociopolitical narratives that dominate settler-Indigenous relations and, more to the point, the colonial nation-state within (and to which) they make those claims. Internal cohesion within a group is one (important) thing, but it is quite another (equally important) thing to have those claims and that identity recognized by groups apart from the group claiming the distinction. Recognition of social and political distinction by dominant settler society is important for Indigenous nation building because a national identity must include a narrative of an Indigenous history that counters that usually forwarded by the colonial nation-state within which we live. For Métis in particular, the fashioning of an internally coherent collective history is key to countering the otherwise dominant Canadian historical narratives, encumbered as they are either in dismissing the very notion of a Métis Nation or consigning us to the dustbin of history as a catalyst for the opening of the nineteenth-century Canadian West.

Nationalist histories and identities are never acontextual, nor do they ever exist outside of the social relations of power within which they are constructed. The benefits that a robust nationalism brings to the process of nation *building* depends on whether others outside that group are (made) aware of—and assent to—the distinction, *and* respect its boundaries; in short, that recognizes it.[29] For any nation-to-nation relationship to be established, all groups must assert and (have) respect(ed) these claims of distinction. This requires groups to exercise a certain level of *epistemic authority* over each other—or at least, a mutual commensurability—sufficient to ensure the meaning of one's own national identity is understood as worthy of distinction. Claims to a national identity rooted in political or cultural difference within already existing *nation-state* boundaries are rarely accepted without contention. In fact, in international relations it is common to see larger domineering states attempt to undermine claims of distinctions within their borders or even neighboring countries.[30]

Discussions about the relationship between nationhood and nation building have failed to account for how Indigenous claims of nationhood are expressed not in a void but in a contentious space where independent and sometimes competing agents possess varying capacities and abilities to have their claims heard, understood, and recognized by others. This makes the concept of *epistemic injustice* particularly useful for examining the different levels of ability that claims to Indigenous nationhood might have for enforcing the meaning and value of those asserted distinctions on others. In her impactful 2007 book, *Epistemic Injustice: The Power and Ethics of Knowing,* Miranda Fricker identifies two types of epistemic injustice relevant to our discussion. Testimonial epistemic injustice takes place when an individual's credibility is unfairly diminished due to prejudice. In the context of making nationalist claims, the notion of hermeneutical injustice proves to be especially valuable.[31] *Hermeneutical injustice* is the result of widespread misunderstanding among a dominant social group that undercuts a marginalized social group's capacity to interpret its own social reality and project this understanding onto the dominant group. For Indigenous Peoples, the phenomenon of hermeneutical injustice often means that collective misunderstandings arise due to the systemic marginalization of Indigenous nationalist claims. This marginalization limits the broader society's ability to accurately comprehend and value Indigenous perspectives on nationhood.[32]

When it comes to the relationship between epistemic injustice and the development of political claims in national forms, hermeneutical injustice occurs when the dominant group in a society unduly controls the narrative of "minority nations'" history and culture and marginalizes the perspectives and knowledge of such collective claims. The next section demonstrates that the Métis are subject to an unequal distribution of symbolic and material resources for participating in the production of knowledge in ways that undermine their claims to nationhood in Canada and further, that the Métis suffer from a form of epistemic injustice distinct from the forms of injustice suffered by other Indigenous nations in Canada.

The Epistemic Marginalization of Métis Claims to Nationhood
Insofar as nations are fundamentally about roots,[33] historical narratives represent a key prong of nation-based arguments.[34] Stuart Hall argues, for example, that the very nature of identity and identity-making involves the use of resources of history to support those claims.[35] Cultural and political actors' claims to nationhood can and do make use of a variety of social/political/historical resources to assert a distinction from other groups. As we will

demonstrate below, however, only certain Indigenous claims in the landscape of a contemporary multinational democracy[36] like Canada resonate, and we argue that important historical reasons exist for why this is the case. That is to say, the "stock" of historical narratives that can be used to persuade is finite. For example: relative to other Indigenous Peoples (and until the 2017 signings of various Métis Nation Accords under the current federal government[37]), Canadians and the Canadian government have consistently failed to hear the *collective* claims of distinction and nationhood emphasized by Métis leaders and communities over the past century and more.

Broader settler society has likewise often met collective Métis assertions of a national distinctiveness with impatience, incredulity, and at certain historical moments, outright dismissal. It is our contention that this gap originates, in part, from narratives of racial ambiguity that have been directed toward the Métis, a position that profoundly shaped the historical manner in which our legal relationships to lands and territories could be considered and consequently deprived of the kinds of epistemic resources crucial to asserting a national distinction, then and today. The following section explores how our intertwined postcontact origins, racial mixedness, and the implications of the scrip system have influenced the treatment of Métis claims to Aboriginal title and identity.

Racial Narratives: A "Mixed" First Nation

The word "*First*" in the phrase "*First Nation*" sets out an important distinction from other minorities in Canada. Unlike other minorities, First Nations have a historical claim to territory and connection to it. In effect, and like treaties, the very term *First Nation* serves to remind Canada that its own history did not begin with the arrival of European settlers and indeed serves as an epistemic resource that supports the idea of Indigenous nationhood for First Nations. Compare this with how the use of the term *Métis* has often become a conceptual placeholder for mixedness among many Canadians.[38]

The Métis are distinct, postcontact Indigenous Peoples with roots in—and routes emanating predominantly (though, given the Métis presence at Fort Edmonton and Pembina, not entirely) from—the historic Red River community.[39] Like other Indigenous Peoples, the Métis collectively represent the sum of distinctive languages, foods, art, dance, kinship networks, legal and governance traditions and, critically, historical and political self-awareness as a collective distinct from Canadians,[40] from Europeans and from other Indigenous nations. Yet Métis political actors' ability to project a Métis nationalist view onto outsiders has been further diminished by the way that view has been subjected to a process of *racialization*. Andersen notes that the Canadian public has largely seen the Métis Nation as a category composed not of a distinct culture, language, and social order but rather of a bunch of racially mixed individuals, or as the offspring of two nations (First Nation and European).[41] This broader narrative of cultural ambivalence has rendered Métis nationhood especially vulnerable to being *misrecognized* as a hybrid offshoot of two races, "Indian" and "white," rather than as an *Indigenous nation*.[42]

Compared to how the term "First Nations" clearly supports such claims to nationhood (albeit also racialized in their own forms), the fact that the word "Métis" (or "metis") often acts as a conceptual placeholder for mixedness— and what this has been taken to mean by Canadian government agencies and the courts for more than a century—means that Métis nationhood must contend with a racialized hierarchy with powerful and enduring political (and policy) consequences. According to such racialized logics, if First Nations are "Indigenous to this land" (and this provides them the moral standing for distinction and self-government)[43] then because only "half" of Métis identity stems from First Nations, the Métis are fractionally less Indigenous and, as a consequence, are less deserving of self-government.[44] Further—and similar to the way that the Métis lack a treaty process—the idea that the Métis are a cultural offshoot more than they are an Indigenous nation unto themselves, denies the Métis Nation a powerful cognitive resource for asserting their distinctiveness unto the broader Canadian consciousness.

Dispossession: Treaties Versus Scrip

In Canada, historical treaties represent a privileged discursive resource of history that supports First Nation claims of distinction today.[45] The fact that treaties represent agreements between nations—the First Nation(s) and the Crown—is highlighted in support of Indigenous distinctiveness today through the popular phrase "we are all treaty people."[46] In fact, the phrase and settler representations of the treatymaking process have steadily become part of the political vernacular in Canada.[47] Treatymaking plays a role in creating a sense of self for Canadians. To wit:

> Modern treaties are a key component of Canadian nation-building. They promote strong and sustainable Aboriginal communities, and create enduring intergovernmental relationships between treaty partners. Further, modern treaties establish certainty with respect to the ownership and management of lands and resources, create a stable climate for investment, and promote broader economic and policy objectives to the benefit of all Canadians.[48]

Treaties provide a common story and a sense of national birth. This offers a powerful cognitive/epistemic apparatus for maintaining national distinctions between Canadians and First Nations. For signatories, a treaty means that "identifying as a nation may be a non-issue. The nation has a continuing and profound historical presence and prominence in the minds of its people."[49] Treaties support external recognition of an Indigenous national identity and root a nation-to-nation relationship in the contemporary vernacular and cognitive landscape of the society at large. Since Métis were never official signatories to historical treaty signings (despite sometimes playing central roles as interpreters during negotiations), they lack the enduring rhetorical power that treaties provide when making claims of a national distinction. In fact, in extinguishing Métis claims to land, the Canadian government did so with the express intent of treating the Métis not as a nation but as individuals, subsumed into the Canadian state. This is clear in a section 31 of the Manitoba Act:

> And whereas, it is expedient, towards the extinguishment of the Indian Title to the lands in the Province, to appropriate a portion of such ungranted lands, to the extent of one million four hundred thousand acres thereof, for the benefit of the families of the half-breed residents, it is hereby enacted, that, under regulations to be from time to time made by the Governor General in Council, the Lieutenant-Governor shall select such lots or tracts in such parts of the Province as he may deem expedient, to the extent aforesaid, and divide the same among the children of the half-breed heads of families residing in the Province at the time of the said transfer to Canada, and the same shall be granted to the said children respectively, in such mode and on such conditions as to settlement and otherwise. as the Governor General in Council may from time to time determine.[50]

Unlike a treaty process, which required the mutual acceptance of terms between different nations, settler-state dealings with the Métis such as those undertaken through the *Manitoba Act,* were a performance on behalf of the Canadian state asserting that it was the only true nation. The Canadian state intended to treat the Métis as a collection of individuals and not as a nation. Likewise, the extinguishment of title was made through a process decided by one party (the Canadian government) and the allotted 1.4 million-acres is distributed at the behest of the governor general. The whole process was an affront to Métis sovereignty with the Canadian government acting as a "benevolent" caretaker.[51] Métis were positioned as problems to be (re)solved rather than as partners to be formally engaged—and treated—with.

It was, however, the practical manner, or system, in which land extinguishment was carried out that has perhaps had the greatest impact on how outsiders think about (the validity of) Métis nationhood. Métis dispossession of lands occurred through an individualization of land title. The Métis were provided land entitlement through scrip[52]—which was offered to the heads of Métis families. Scrip was a certificate issued by the federal government that allowed Métis (or representatives of Métis, such as land speculators) to receive money or homestead lands upon presentation of the document to the Dominion Lands Office. The result, even when it worked as ostensibly organized, was that Métis families were granted parcels of land disconnected from each other. Each scrip certificate was provided to an individual not community or nation. The aim was clearly to treat the Métis people as charges of the Canadian state and not as a nation unto their own. The *Manitoba Act* was a unilateral action of the Canadian Parliament in many ways. It is not a treaty between independent partners.[53]

While the scrip and treaty system were both designed to extinguish Indigenous legal relationships to land, they fail to provide the same leverage as an epistemic resource for enforcing a national identity. Treaties are better able to help enforce the idea that First Nations are discrete nations, not least because First Nations emphasize them as a source of their legal rights and their nation-ness as does the Canadian government and its various ministries.[54] For the Métis, the scrip system effectively undermined Métis nation-ness insofar as the entire extinguishment process used to consider Métis claims treated the Métis as *not* a nation, but as individuals.[55] Scrip was part of a strategic move by the Canadian state to deal with Métis claims (to legally consider "Half-breed title" in the parlance of the day). Today, its contemporary symbolic resonances narrow the way Métis can assert a national distinction. In short, such historical administrative decisions structurally prejudice the understanding of the Métis as a collective in collective Canadian understanding. And, although more recent court decisions[56] have rhetorically noted these historical injustices, their eventual policy impact remains unclear.

The Epistemic Landscape Facing Métis Nation- Building

The environment in which Métis national identity is expressed has left the Métis at an epistemic disadvantage in terms of enforcing their preferred meaning and value of the word "Métis" vis-à-vis Canadian consciousness. This epistemic landscape not only leaves the Métis vulnerable to outsiders rejecting the notion of a distinct Métis nation but also allows outsiders to define for themselves what it means to be Métis (and more to the point, whether they are themselves Métis, despite the lack of historical consciousness as such). At the individual level, a growing number of "identity fraud" cases (particularly in the academy) have centered on individuals who have used claims to a Métis identity to access educational and professional opportunities.[57] Similarly, but on a more macro level, the inability of the Métis to enforce the notion of their own distinction onto the Canadian consciousness have likewise permitted some non-Métis the ability (if not to say the possessive entitlement) to define who they believe the Métis are. For example, in his 2008 bestseller, *A Fair Country,* John Ralston Saul argues that contemporary Canada has been deeply influenced and shaped by Aboriginal and European ideas and experience for over 250 years. Indeed, it is the mixing of these two different experiences, Saul informs us, that Canada and all Canadians are part of what he refers to as a "métis civilization":

> We are a métis civilization. What we are today has been inspired as much by four centuries of life with the indigenous civilizations as by four centuries of immigration. Perhaps more. Today we are the outcome of that experience. As have Métis people, Canadians in general have been heavily influenced and shaped by the First Nations.[58]

Saul's logic represents yet another example of the Métis being *misrecognized* as a hybrid offshoot of two races—"Indian" and "white," rather than as an *Indigenous* people. More broadly, it is another example of the vulnerability of Métis nationhood vis-à-vis non-Métis constructions of what it is to be Métis. Saul's framing of Canada as a métis civilization" is an argument made possible only because *he is able* to also ignore or downplay the ethnogenesis story of the Métis as a distinct nation. Saul's enforcement of the notion that Métis are "mixed" or "hybrid" is not new. Nor is the process of appropriation. This process of non-Métis people defining for themselves what it is to be Métis to advance their own arguments has directly resulted in obstacles to Métis self-governance. The Métis have had a difficult time enforcing a preferred meaning and value of their distinction on outsiders. When Saul defines the Métis, he does so as a racial and not nationally cultural group and this in turn creates the limits then used to argue against the Métis aspirations for political agency. But what is important to note here, is that when Saul (and others) use their own definitions of the Métis to advance their own ideas, their ability and willingness to do so derives from the way that the Métis, as an Indigenous nation, is more broadly structurally prejudiced by a deep cavity in the well of Canadian collective understanding.

Conclusion

Over the past four decades, Indigenous political claims have increasingly taken a nationalist form—sometimes "again" (as is the case with Métis claims), sometimes newly so (according to Paul Nadasdy,[59] this is the case among First Nations in the Yukon). While this approach acknowledges that Indigenous Peoples' claims to nationhood hinge upon a distinct separation between their communities and those of settlers being recognized by external entities, it fails to consider how and the extent to which: (1) nationhood and assertions of national distinctiveness are fundamentally claims-based activities that take place *in competition* with others; and (2) that different actors possess varying capabilities to enforce or support such claims.

Throughout the article, we emphasized the power of nation-states to set the parameters within which individuals and collectivities claim—and can claim—their identities. In this context, we argued Métis claims to nationhood are caught on the horns of, on the one hand, a contemporary Canadian recognition of the general validity of Indigenous nationhood and, on the other, a set of historical legal/administrative decisions—in addition to the absorption by the nascent Canadian nation-state of prevailing racial grammars inherited from British imperialism—that symbolically placed Métis claims to collective solidarity "below" those of other Indigenous claims to nationhood. Therefore, before concluding that nationhood offers these advantages for nation building, it is necessary to determine the extent to which—and even, in some cases, whether—a nation can symbolically enforce its claim. Given the legal-administrative decisions that Canadian state authorities chose to deal with "Indigenous" inhabitants during its early formation, the Métis in particular have largely lacked this ability, and the concept of epistemic injustice—specifically hermeneutical injustice—effectively illustrates how widespread misunderstandings among a dominant social group (a colonial, largely "whitestream" Canada) undermines our capacity to interpret our own social reality and convey this understanding to the dominant group. Indeed, having our cultural distinction recognized by non-Métis often runs up against external and imposed conceptions of who we are and this, in turn, can pose a threat to the nation-(re)building process. Being racialized as a "mixed-group" with little to no ethno-genesis story, or having land disposed through a process that effectively individualized/de-collectivized the nation, are each part of a broader colonial legacy distinctive to the Métis and one that must be overcome in Métis nation-building processes.

KURTIS BOYER is a political scientist working in the areas of Indigenous governance and political psychology. He is currently an assistant professor at the Johnson-Shoyama Graduate School of Public Policy, University of Saskatchewan. He is a Chair in Métis Governance and Policy and a Lafond-Molloy Fellow in Leadership and Innovation in Indigenous Governance at The Institute for Research on Public Policy (IRRP)

CHRIS ANDERSEN is dean of the Faculty of Native Studies at the University of Alberta. He is the author of two books including, with Maggie Walter, *Indigenous Statistics: A Quantitative Indigenous Methodology* (2013) and *"Métis": Race, Recognition and the Struggle for Indigenous Peoplehood* (2014). In 2023, he was named as a Fellow of the Boundaries, Membership & Belonging Program, Canadian Institute for Advanced Research.

References

Adese, Jennifer, and Chris Andersen, eds. *A People and a Nation: New Directions in Contemporary Métis Studies.* Vancouver: UBC Press, 2021.

Alfred, Gerald. *Heeding the Voices of Our Ancestors: Kahnawake and the Rise of Native Nationalism.* Don Mills: Oxford University Press, 1995.

Alfred, Taiaiake. *Peace, Power, Righteousness: An Indigenous Manifesto.* New York: Oxford University Press, 2009.

Akee, Randall. "Sovereignty and Improved Economic Outcomes for American Indians: Building on the Gains Made since 1990." Washington Centre for Equitable Growth, January 14, 2021. https://equitablegrowth.org/sovereignty-and-improved-economic-outcomes-for-american-indians-building-on-the-gains-made-since-1990/.

Andersen, Chris. *"Métis": Race, Recognition, and the Struggle for Indigenous Peoplehood.* Vancouver: UBC Press, 2014.

Anderson, Benedict. *Imagined Communities: Reflections on the Origin and Spread of Nationalism.* New York: Verso, 2006.

Banting, Keith, Allison Harell, and Will Kymlicka. "Nationalism, Membership, and the Politics of Minority Claims-Making." *Canadian Journal of Political Science* 55, no. 3 (2022): 537–60.

Berthelette, Scott. *Heirs of an Ambivalent Empire: French-Indigenous Relations and the Rise of the Métis in the Hudson Bay Watershed.* Montreal and Kingston: McGill-Queen's Press, 2022.

Braudel, Fernand. *Civilization and Capitalism, 15th-18th Century, Vol. III: The Perspective of the World.* Translated by Siân Reynold. Berkeley: University of California Press, 1992.

Bloemraad, Irene. "Theorizing the Power of Citizenship as Claims-Making." *Journal of Ethnic and Migration Studies* 44, no. 1 (2018): 4–26.

Bonikowski, Bart. "Ethno-Nationalist Populism and the Mobilization of Collective Resentment." *British Journal of Sociology* 68, S1 (2017): S181–S213.

Brubaker, Rogers. "In the Name of the Nation: Reflections on Nationalism and Patriotism." *Citizenship Studies* 8, no. 2 (2004): 115–27.

Boyer, Kurtis, and Paul Simard. "Self-Indigenization as Epistemic Injustice" In *Métis Coming Together,* edited by Laura Forsythe and Jennifer Markides. Bristol: Peter Lang. Forthcoming.

Brubaker, Rogers. *Nationalism Reframed: Nationhood and the National Question in the New Europe.* Cambridge: Cambridge University Press, 1996.

Carvalho, Susana, and Francois Gemenne eds., *Nations and Their Histories: Constructions and Representations*. New York: Palgrave Macmillan, 2009.

Chartrand, L. A. H. "Aboriginal Rights: The Dispossession of the Métis." *Osgoode Hall Law Journal* 29, no. 3 (1991): 457–82.

Corntassel, Jeff, and Richard Witmer. *Forced Federalism: Contemporary Challenges to Indigenous Nationhood*. Norman: University of Oklahoma Press, 2008.

Corrigan, Derek, and Philip Sayer. *The Great Arch: State Formation, Cultural Revolution, and the Rise of Capitalism*. New York: Basil Blackwell, 1985.

Cornell, Stephen. "Processes of Native Nationhood: The Indigenous Politics of Self-Government." *International Indigenous Policy Journal* 6, no. 4 (September 9, 2015): 4.

Coulthard, Glen Sean. *Red Skin, White Masks: Rejecting the Colonial Politics of Recognition*. Minneapolis: University of Minnesota Press, 2014.

Daniels v. Canada (Indian Affairs and Northern Development), 2016 SCC 12, [2016] 1 S.C.R. 99.

Dennison, Jean. *Vital Relations: How the Osage Nation Moves Indigenous Nationhood into the Future*. Chapel Hill: University of North Carolina Press, 2024.

Devine, Heather. *The People Who Own Themselves: Aboriginal Ethnogenesis in a Canadian Family, 1660–1900*. Calgary: University of Calgary Press, 2012.

Diaz, Vincente. "Voyaging for Anti-Colonial Recovery: Austronesian Seafaring, Archipelagic Rethinking, and Re-mapping Indigeneity." *Pacific Asia Inquiry* 2, no. 1 (2011): 21–32.

Downey, Allen. *The Creator's Game: Lacrosse, Identity, and Indigenous Nationhood*. Vancouver: UBC Press, 2018.

Fricker, Miranda. *Epistemic Injustice: The Power and Ethics of Knowing*. New York: Oxford University Press, 2007.

Flanagan, Thomas. "Ottawa Made a Promise to the Métis Nation—But They Shouldn't Keep It." *The Globe and Mail*. September 12, 2017. https://www.theglobeandmail.com/opinion/ottawa-made-a-promise-to-the-Métis-nation-but-they-shouldnt-keep-it/article36233269/.

Gaudry, Adam. "*Kaa-tipeyimishoyaahk*—'We Are Those Who Own Ourselves': A Political History of Métis Self-Determination in the North-West, 1830–1870." PhD diss., University of Victoria, 2014.

Gaudry, Adam. "New Métis, Métis Identity Appropriation, and the Displacement of Living Métis Culture." *American Indian Quarterly* 42, no. 2 (2018): 162–90.

Gaudry, Adam, and Chris Andersen. "Daniels v. Canada: Racialized Legacies, Settler Self-Indigenization and the Denial of Indigenous Peoplehood." *TOPIA: Canadian Journal of Cultural Studies* 36 (2016): 19–30.

Gellner, Ernest. *Nations and Nationalism*. Ithaca, NY: Cornell University Press, 1983.

Government of Canada. n.d. "Archived—An Act to Amend and Continue the Act 32 and 33 Victoria, Chapter 3 ; and to Establish and Provide for the Government of the Province of Manitoba, S.C. 1870, c. 3." Accessed March 1, 2024. https://www.sac-isc.gc.ca/eng/1100100010208/1618941272137.

———. n.d. "Canada-Métis Nation Accord." Prime Minister of Canada. Accessed January 11, 2024. https://www.pm.gc.ca/en/canada-Métis-nation-accord.

———. n.d. "Implementation of Modern Treaties and Self-government Agreements." Accessed July 11, 2024. https://www.rcaanc-cirnac.gc.ca/eng/15732 25148041/1573225175098.

———. n.d. "Modern Treaties Are a Key Component of Canadian Nation-Building." Accessed January 11, 2024. https://www.rcaanc-cirnac.gc.ca/eng /1436288286602/1677261996355#chp1.

——— .n.d. "Statement of Principles on the Federal Approach to Modern Treaty Implementation." Accessed June 11, 2024. https://www.rcaanc-cirnac.gc.ca /eng/1436288286602/1677261996355#chp1.

Giddens, Anthony. *A Contemporary Critique of Historical Materialism, Vol. 1: Power, Property and the State.* Cambridge: Polity, 1981.

Hall, Patrick. "Nationalism and Historicit." *Nations and Nationalism* 3, no. 1 (1997): 3–23.

Hall, Stuart. "The Question of Cultural Identity." In *Modernity: An Introduction to Modern Societies,* edited by Stuart Hall, David Held, Don Hubert, and Kenneth Thompson, 264–89. Cambridge: Polity Press, 1995.

Hall, Stuart, and Paul du Gay. *Questions of Cultural Identity.* London: SAGE, 2011.

Hall, Stuart. "Nations and Diasporas." In *The Fateful Triangle: Race, Ethnicity, Nation,* edited by Kobena Mercer. Cambridge, MA: Harvard University Press, 2017.

Hobsbawm, Eric J. *Nations and Nationalism since 1780: Programme, Myth, Reality.* Cambridge: Cambridge University Press, 1990.

Hobsbawm, Eric J., and Terence Ranger. *The Invention of Tradition.* Cambridge: Cambridge University Press, 2012.

Indigenous Services Canada. "Archived—An Act to Amend and Continue the Act 32 and 33 Victoria, Chapter 3 ; and to Establish and Provide for the Government of the Province of Manitoba, S.C. 1870, c. 3." Legislation and Regulations. Last modified September 15, 2010. https://www.sac-isc.gc.ca/eng /1100100010208/1618941272137.

Keating, Michael. *Plurinational Democracy: Stateless Nations in a Post-sovereignty Era.* Oxford: Oxford University Press, 2001.

Kolopenuk, Jessica. "The Pretendian Problem." *Canadian Journal of Political Science* 56, no. 2 (June 2023): 468–73.

Kuman, Krishan. "Nationalism and the Historians." In *The SAGE Handbook of Nations and Nationalism,* edited by Gerard Delanty and Krishan Kumar, 7–20. London: SAGE, 2006.

Kuzio, Taras. "Identity and Nation-Building in Ukraine: Defining the 'Other.'" *Ethnicities* 1, no. 3 (2001): 343–65.

Kymlicka, Will. *Multicultural Citizenship: A Liberal Theory of Minority Rights.* Oxford: Clarendon Press, 1996.

Leroux, Darryl. *White Claims to Indigenous Identity.* Winnipeg: University of Manitoba Press, 2019.

Linz, Juan José. "State Building and Nation Building." *European Review* 1 (1993): 355–69.

MacDougall, Brenda. *Contours of a People: Métis Family, Mobility, and History.* Norman: University of Oklahoma Press, 2012.

———. "How We Know Who We Are: Historical Literacy, Kinscapes, and Defining a People." In *Daniels v. Canada: In and beyond the Courts,* edited by Nathalie Kermoal and Chris Andersen, 233–267. Winnipeg: University of Manitoba Press, 2021.

Manitoba Métis Federation Inc. v. Canada (Attorney General), 2013 SCC 14, [2013] 1 S.C.R. 623.

McKenzie-Jones, Paul. "What Does 'We Are All Treaty People' Mean, and Who Speaks for Indigenous Students on Campus?" *The Conversation,* August 29, 2019. http://theconversation.com/what-does-we-are-all-treaty-people-mean-and-who-speaks-for-indigenous-students-on-campus-119060.

Nadasdy, Paul. "Boundaries among Kin: Sovereignty, the Modern Treaty Process, and the Rise of Ethno-Territorial Nationalism among Yukon First Nations." *Comparative Studies in Society and History* 54, no. 3 (2012): 499–532.

OECD. "Linking Indigenous Communities with Regional Development in Canada." accessed February 18, 2022. https://www.oecd-ilibrary.org/sites/e6cc8722-en/index.html?itemId=/content/component/e6cc8722-en.

O'Toole, Darren, "From Entity to Identity to Nation: The Ethnogenesis of the Wiisakodewininiwag (Bois-Brûlés) Reconsidered." In *The Métis in Canada,* edited by Christopher Adams, Gregg Dahl and Ian Peach. Edmonton: University of Alberta Press, 2013.

O'Toole, Darren. "Manitoba Métis Federation Inc. v. Canada: Breathing New Life into the 'Empty Box' Doctrine of 'Indian Title.'" *Alberta Law Review* 52, no. 3 (2015): 674.

Peterson, Jacqueline, and Jennifer Brown, eds. *The New People: Being and Becoming Métis in North America.* Winnipeg: University of Manitoba Press, 1985.

Robbins, Richard, and Rachel Dowty. *Global Problems and the Culture of Capitalism, Books a La Carte.* 7th ed. New York: Pearson, 2018.

Simpson, Audra. "Paths toward a Mohawk Nation: Narratives of Citizenship and Nationhood in Kahnawake." In *Political Theory and the Rights of Indigenous Peoples,* edited by Duncan Ivison, Paul Patton, and William Sanders, 113–36. Cambridge: Cambridge University Press, 2000.

———. *Mohawk Interruptus: Political Life Across the Borders of Settler States.* Durham, N.C.: Duke University Press, 2014.

St-Onge, Nicole, Carolyn Podruchny, and Brenda MacDougall. *Contours of a People: Métis Family, Mobility, and History.* New Directions in Native American Studies. Norman: University of Oklahoma Press, 2012.

Taylor, Jonathan. "Determinants of Development Success in the Native Nations of the United States." Native Nations Institute for Leadership, Management, and Policy. Last modified 2008. https://nnigovernance.arizona.edu/determinants-development-success-native-nations-united-states-english.

Tough, Frank. *'As Their Natural Resources Fail': Native Peoples and the Economic History of Northern Manitoba, 1870–1930.* Vancouver: UBC Press, 1996.

Simeone, Tonina. *The Harvard Project on American Indian Economic Develop-ment: Findings and Considerations.* Ottawa: Parliamentary Information and Research Service: Political and Social Affairs Division, 2007.

Tilly, Charles. *The Formation of National States in Western Europe.* Princeton, N.J.: Princeton University Press, 1975.

Tsosie, Rebecca. "Indigenous Peoples, Anthropology, and the Legacy of Epis-temic Injustice." In *The Routledge Handbook of Epistemic Injustice,* edited by Ian James Kidd, José Medina, and Gaile Pohlhaus Jr., 356–69. New York: Routledge, 2017.

Saul, John Ralston. *A Fair Country: Telling Truths About Canada.* Toronto: Pen-guin Canada, 2009.

Voth, Daniel. "The Choices We Make and the World They Create: Métis Conflicts With Treaty 1 Peoples in MMF v. Canada." *University of Toronto Law Journal* 68, no. 3 (2018): 358–400.

Wacquant, Löic. "For an Analytic of Racial Domination." *Political Power and Social Theory* 11, (1997): 222–34.

Weber, Eugene. "Nationalism and the Politics of Resentment." *American Scholar* 63, no. 3 (1994): 421–28.

Weber, Max. *Economy and Society: An Outline of Interpretive Sociology.* 2 vols. Berkeley: University of California Press, 1978.

Notes

1. Stephen Cornell, "Processes of Native Nationhood: The Indigenous Poli-tics of Self-Government," *International Indigenous Policy Journal* 6, no. 4 (Sep-tember 9, 2015): 4.

2. When referring to "others" in our discussion, we primarily mean the Canadian general public. However, it's important to note that various Indig-enous nations have contested the Indigenous status of the Métis. For an in-depth exploration of the Métis conflicts with Treaty 1 Peoples, particularly in the context of the *Manitoba Métis Federation v. Canada* case, see Daniel Voth, "The Choices We Make and the World They Create: Métis Conflicts with Treaty 1 Peoples in *MMF v. Canada,*" *University of Toronto Law Journal,* 68, no. 3 (Sum-mer 2018): 358–80. This analysis includes a detailed examination of the inter-vener factum submitted by Treaty No. 1 First Nations during the appellate court proceedings.

3. Juan José Linz. "State Building and Nation Building," *European Review* 1 (1993): 355–69; Philip Corrigan and Derek Sayer, *The Great Arch: English State Formation as Cultural Revolution,* New York: Blackwell, 1985: 7; Rogers Brubaker, "In the Name of the Nation: Reflections on Nationalism and Patrio-tism," *Citizenship Studies* 8, no. 2 (June 2004): 115–27.

4. Kurtis Boyer and Paul Simard, "Self-Indigenization as Epistemic Injus-tice," *Métis Coming Together,* ed. Laura Forsythe and Jennifer Markides (Bristol: Peter Lang, forthcoming).

5. See Jennifer Adese and Chris Andersen, eds., *A People and a Nation: New Directions in Contemporary Métis Studies* (Vancouver: UBC Press, 2021); Chris

Andersen, *"Métis": Race, Recognition, and the Struggle for Indigenous Peoplehood.* (Vancouver: UBC Press, 2014); Nicole St-Onge, Carolyn Podruchny, and Brenda MacDougall, *Contours of a People: Métis Family, Mobility, and History, New Directions in Native American Studies,* Norman: University of Oklahoma Press, 2012; Nicole St-Onge, "Plains Métis People: Contours of an Identity," *Australasian Canadian Studies,* 27, no. 1–2 (2009): 95–115.

6. See: Brenda MacDougall, "How We Know Who We Are: Historical Literacy, Kinscapes, and Defining a People," in *Daniels v. Canada: In and beyond the Courts,* 233–67, Winnipeg: University of Manitoba Press, 2021; Andersen, *"Métis": Race, Recognition and the Struggle for Indigenous Peoplehood.*

7. In "Ottawa made a promise to the Métis Nation—but they shouldn't keep it," published in *The Globe and Mail,* Flanagan oversimplifies Métis identity to demographic trends and conjectural incentives, demonstrating a superficial grasp of the complexities surrounding Métis nationhood. This approach not only distorts Métis identity but also detracts from the legitimacy of their self-determination efforts. See: Thomas Flanagan, "Ottawa made a promise to the Métis Nation—but they shouldn't keep it," *Globe and Mail,* September 12, 2017, accessed January 11, 2024, https://www.theglobeandmail.com/opinion /ottawa-made-a-promise-to-the--nation-but-they-shouldnt-keep-it/article 36233269/.

8. The concept of "differential citizenship" underscores the unique legal rights of Indigenous Peoples within Canada's framework. This paper focuses on the Métis, detailing their specific challenges in actualizing self-governance and rights amid legal ambiguities, political resistance, and diverse interpretations of Indigenous entitlements. Given the Métis' distinct colonial experience, this analysis is deliberately centered on them, considering an exploration of other Indigenous groups beyond the scope of this study. Despite theoretical advantages, the Métis' case illustrates the complexities of enacting 'differential citizenship' within their unique historical and sociopolitical landscape. See Will Kymlicka, *Multicultural Citizenship: A Liberal Theory of Minority Rights,* Reprint ed. (Oxford: Clarendon Press, 1996).

9. On the relationship between "minority" claims-making and citizenship more generally, see Rogers Brubaker, *Nationalism Reframed: Nationhood and the National Question in the New Europe* (Cambridge: Cambridge University Press, 1996); Michael Keating, *Plurinational Democracy: Stateless Nations in a Postsovereignty Era* (Oxford: Oxford University Press, 2001). Also see Keith Banting, Allison Harell, and Will Kymlicka, "Nationalism, Membership and the Politics of Minority Claims-Making," *Canadian Journal of Political Science* 55, issue 3 (2022): 537–560; Irene Bloemraad, "Theorizing the Power of Citizenship as Claims-Making." *Journal of Ethnic and Migration Studies* 44, no. 1 (2018): 4–26.

10. Löic Wacquant, "For an Analytic of Racial Domination," *Political Power and Social Theory* 11 (1997): 222.

11. On the tendency of scholars of nationalism to see nations as "things," see Brubaker, *Nationalism Reframed,* ch. 1.

12. See: Benedict Anderson, *Imagined Communities: Reflections on the Origin and Spread of Nationalism* (New York: Verso, 2006); Ernest Gellner, *Nations*

and Nationalism (Ithaca: Cornell University Press, 1983); Eric J. Hobsbawm, *Nations and Nationalism since 1780: Programme, Myth, Reality* (Cambridge: Cambridge University Press, 1990); Stuart Hall, "The question of cultural identity," in *Modernity: An introduction to modern societies,* ed. Stuart Hall, David Held, Don Hubert, and Kenneth Thompson, 595–634. Cambridge: Polity Press, 1995. In the context of taking for granted the Métis nation as a "group" and in that context, exploring the various ways that "it" has been oppressed, the field is now voluminous. See various contributions in the edited collection Jennifer Adese and Chris Andersen, eds., *A People and a Nation: New Directions in Contemporary Métis Studies* (Vancouver: UBC Press, 2021); Chris Andersen, *"Métis": Race, Recognition, and the Struggle for Indigenous Peoplehood*; Heather Devine, *The People Who Own Themselves: Aboriginal Ethnogenesis in a Canadian Family, 1660–1900* (Calgary: University of Calgary Press, 2012); Adam Gaudry, *Kaa-tipeyimishoyaahk*—"We Are Those Who Own Ourselves': A Political History of Métis Self-Determination in the North-West, 1830–1870, (PhD diss., University of Victoria, 2014); Jacqueline Peterson and Jennifer Brown, eds., *The New People: Being and Becoming Métis in North America* (Winnipeg: University of Manitoba Press, 1985); O'Toole, Darren, "From Entity to Identity to Nation: The Ethnogenesis of the Wiisakodewininiwag (Bois-Brûlés) Reconsidered," in *The Métis in Canada,* ed. Christopher Adams, Gregg Dahl and Ian Peach (Edmonton: University of Alberta Press, 2013), 143–203. Additionally, Daniel Voth's analysis on Métis legal and political struggles offers an insightful perspective into the complexities of Métis identity and rights claims within Canada. See Daniel Voth, "The Choices We Make and the World They Create: Métis Conflicts with Treaty 1 Peoples in MMF v. Canada," *The University of Toronto Law Journal,* 68, no. 3 (Summer 2018): 358–80. It is important to note that our approach here is not intended as a critique of this literature, much of which has been written by Métis scholars. Rather, we begin from a different ontological perspective to better investigate the manner in which Métis political actors (are able to) make national *claims* today.

13. Some of the key differences between the primordialist and modernist camps were laid out in the so-called Warwick Debates between a leading proponent of each camp: Earnst Gellner in the modernist camp and his former student, Anthony Smith, in the primordialist camp. See Anthony Smith, "Opening Statement: Nations and Their Pasts," *Nations and Nationalism* 2, no. 3 (1996); Earnst Gellner, "Reply: Do Nations Have Navels?" *Nations and Nationalism* 2, no. 3 (1996); and Anthony Smith, "Memory and modernity: Reflections on E. Gellner's Theory of Nationalism," *Nations and Nationalism* 2, no. 3 (1996).

14. See Anthony Giddens, *A Contemporary Critique of Historical Materialism, Vol. 1: Power, Property and the State* (Cambridge: Polity, 1981), 172.

15. Charles Tilly, *The Formation of National States in Western Europe* (Princeton, N.J.: Princeton University Press, 1975).

16. Fernand Braudel, *Civilization and Capitalism, 15th-18th Century, Vol. III: The Perspective of the World,* trans. Siân Reynold (Berkeley: University of California Press, 1992), 515–6. Also see Max Weber, *Economy and Society: An Outline of Interpretive Sociology,* 2 vols. (Berkeley: University of California Press, 1978).

17. Richard Robbins and Rachel Dowty, *Global Problems and the Culture of Capitalism, Books a La Carte*, 7th ed. (New York: Pearson, 2018) 104.

18. Eric J. Hobsbawm and Terence Ranger, "Introduction: Inventing Traditions," in *The Invention of Tradition*, ed. Eric J. Hobsbawm and Terence Ranger (Cambridge: Cambridge University Press, 2012: 1), 1–14.

19. Philip Corrigan and Derek Sayer, *The Great Arch: State Formation, Cultural Revolution and the Rise of Capitalism* (New York: Basil Blackwell, 1985), 3. We might also think about the power of state institutions as "sites of epistemic authority" or as Pierre Bourdieu once termed it, "a central bank of symbolic capital"; see Pierre Bourdieu and Loic Wacquant, "From Ruling Class to Field of Power: An Interview with Pierre Bourdieu on La Noblesse d'État," *Theory, Culture & Society* 10, no. 3 (August 1993): 39–40.

20. Philip Corrigan and Derek Sayer, *The Great Arch: State Formation, Cultural Revolution and the Rise of Capitalism*, 3.

21. Stuart Hall, "The Question of Cultural Identity," in *Modernity: An Introduction to Modern Societies*, edited by Stuart Hall, David Held, Don Hubert, and Kenneth Thompson, 264–89 (Cambridge: Polity Press, 1995). Also see Stuart Hall, "Nations and Diasporas," in *The Fateful Triangle: Race, Ethnicity, Nation*, ed. Kobena Mercer (Cambridge, Mass.: Harvard University Press, 2017).

22. Though Hall speaks in terms of a "national culture" rather than specifically speaking to the power of the nation-state, his analysis (can) clearly incorporate the elemental cultural power of the state, with its ability to (re)produce the apparent naturalness of the key elements of the nation it claims and in doing so, to offer a depiction of the nation as a form of cultural unity more or less coterminous with its geopolitical efforts at boundary-making.

23. Brubaker, *Nationalism Reframed*, 63.

24. Andersen, *"Métis": Race, Recognition, and the Struggle for Indigenous Peoplehood*, 93; also see Hall, "Nations and Diasporas," 142.

25. Though beyond the scope of this article, it is nonetheless worth asking why nationalism in particular (as opposed to other forms of collective solidarity or belonging) has become so naturalized as a system of political and cultural representation (see Rogers Brubaker, "Charles Tilly as a Theorist of Nationalism," *The American Sociologist* 41 (2010): 375–81). Also see Paul Nadasdy, "Boundaries among Kin: Sovereignty, the Modern Treaty Process, and the Rise of Ethno-Territorial Nationalism among Yukon First Nations," *Comparative Studies in Society and History* 54, no. 3 (2012): 499–532.

26. See Gerald Alfred, *Heeding the Voices of Our Ancestors: Kahnawake and the Rise of Native Nationalism* (Don Mills: Oxford University Press, 1995), 14.

27. Audra Simpson, *Mohawk Interruptus: Political Life Across the Borders of Settler States* (Durham, N.C.: Duke University Press, 2014), 11.

28. Indigenous nationhood as a concept has been discussed at length elsewhere. This literature is now voluminous but see the following for a sense of some of the contexts within which Indigenous nationalism has been deployed: Alfred, *Heeding the Voices of our Ancestors*; Taiaiake Alfred, *Peace, Power, Righteousness: An Indigenous Manifesto* (New York: Oxford University Press, 2009); Jeff Corntassel and Richard Witmer, *Forced Federalism: Contemporary*

Challenges to Indigenous Nationhood (Norman: University of Oklahoma Press, 2008); Glen Sean Coulthard, *Red Skin, White Masks: Rejecting the Colonial Politics of Recognition* (Minneapolis: University of Minnesota Press, 2014); Jean Dennison, *Vital Relations: How the Osage Nation Moves Indigenous Nationhood into the Future* (Chapel Hill: University of North Carolina Press, 2024); Allen Downey, *The Creator's Game: Lacrosse, Identity, and Indigenous Nationhood* (Vancouver: UBC Press, 2018; Audra Simpson, "Paths toward a Mohawk Nation: Narratives of Citizenship and Nationhood in Kahnawake," in *Political Theory and the Rights of Indigenous Peoples,* ed. Duncan Ivison, Paul Patton, and William Sanders (Cambridge: Cambridge University Press, 2000), 113–36.

29. Also see Bloemraad, "Theorizing," 14–15 for a more general discussion of the relationship between claims-making and recognition. We are centrally interested in how it relates to a distinct political process Indigenous leaders are increasingly using for politically mobilizing themselves in the pursuit of self-government within Canada.

30. Taras Kuzio, "Identity and Nation-Building in Ukraine: Defining the 'Other,'" *Ethnicities* 1, no. 3 (September 1, 2001): 343–65.

31. Miranda Fricker, *Epistemic Injustice: The Power and Ethics of Knowing* (New York: Oxford University Press, 2007): 1.

32. Rebecca Tsosie, "Indigenous Peoples, Anthropology, and the Legacy of Epistemic Injustice," in *The Routledge Handbook of Epistemic Injustice* (London: Routledge, 2017).

33. Though see Vincente Diaz's brilliant discussion on the possible resonances between nationalism and *routes:* Vincente Diaz, "Voyaging for Anti-Colonial Recovery: Austronesian Seafaring, Archipelagic Rethinking, and Re-mapping Indigeneity," *Pacific Asia Inquiry* 2, no. 1 (2011): 21–32.

34. See Susana Carvalho and Francois Gemenne, eds., *Nations and Their Histories: Constructions and Representations* (New York: Palgrave Macmillan, 2009); Krishan Kuman, "Nationalism and the Historians," in *The SAGE Handbook of Nations and Nationalism,* ed. Gerard Delanty and Krishan Kumar (London: SAGE, 2006), 7–20; Patrick Hall, "Nationalism and Historicity," *Nations and Nationalism* 3, no. 1 (1997): 3–23.

35. Stuart Hall, "Introduction: Who Needs 'Identity'?" in *Questions of Cultural Identity,* (London: SAGE, 2011), 1–17. http://doi.org/10.4135/9781446221907.

36. For a more in-depth discussion of the idea of a "multination democracy," see Will Kymlicka, "Multicultural Citizenship Within Multination States," *Ethnicities* 11, no. 3 (2011): 281–302; Will Kymlicka, *Politics in the Vernacular: Nationalism, Multiculturalism and Citizenship* (Oxford: Oxford University Press, 2001).

37. "Canada-Métis Nation Accord," Prime Minister of Canada, Government of Canada, accessed January 11, 2024, https://www.pm.gc.ca/en/canada -Métis-nation-accord.

38. Chris Andersen, *"Métis": Race, Recognition, and the Struggle for Indigenous Peoplehood.*

39. Chris Andersen, *"Métis": Race, Recognition, and the Struggle for Indigenous Peoplehood,* 27; St-Onge, "Plains Métis People: Contours of an Identity."

40. See Scott Berthelette, *Heirs of an Ambivalent Empire: French-Indigenous Relations and the Rise of the Métis in the Hudson Bay Watershed* (Montreal and Kingston: McGill-Queen's Press, 2022) for a discussion of the early role of Canadien traders in setting the stage for the birth and growth of a Métis national consciousness.

41. Chris Andersen, *"Métis": Race, Recognition, and the Struggle for Indigenous Peoplehood*, 6.

42. Brenda MacDougall, "The Myth of Métis Cultural Ambivalence," in *Contours of a People: Métis Family, Mobility, and History* (Norman: University of Oklahoma Press, 2012).

43. Arguably two of the most important court decisions on this point are *R. v. Calder* (1996),1 S.C.R. 660 and *Delgamuukw v. British Columbia*, (1997) 3 S.C.R. 1010.

44. Chris Andersen, *"Métis": Race, Recognition, and the Struggle for Indigenous Peoplehood*, 7.

45. In certain cases, Indigenous nations the Canadian state categorizes as First Nations whose ancestors did not sign treaties (such as in British Columbia or north of the sixtieth parallel), have had access to a comprehensive land claims/modern treaty process (as inequitable as this may be in its actual practice): "Implementation of modern treaties and self-government agreements," Government of Canada, accessed July 11, 2024, https://www.rcaanc-cirnac .gc.ca/eng/1573225148041/1573225175098. Indeed, the Government of Canada positions this process, as well as the treaty-making modality that is centered within it—as a key part of Canadian nation building. see "Statement of Principles on the Federal Approach to Modern Treaty Implementation," Government of Canada, accessed June 11, 2024, https://www.rcaanc-cirnac.gc.ca/eng/14362 88286602/1677261996355#chp1.

46. Our discussion of treaties references the widespread perception within Canadian society. While our assertion is that the common perception may provide First Nations a degree of epistemic authority, relative to the Métis, this perception may not fully capture the complexity of treaty relationships. This includes acknowledging that not all First Nations have treaty agreements. Moreover, our focus on this common perception does not extend to exploring the viewpoints of Métis leaders regarding the Manitoba Act and whether they regarded it as a form of treaty.

47. Paul McKenzie-Jones, "What Does 'We Are All Treaty People' Mean, and Who Speaks for Indigenous Students on Campus?" *The Conversation*, August 29, 2019, http://theconversation.com/what-does-we-are-all-treaty-people-mean -and-who-speaks-for-indigenous-students-on-campus-119060.

48. "Modern treaties are a key component of Canadian nation-building," Government of Canada, accessed January 11, 2024, https://www.rcaanc-cirnac .gc.ca/eng/1436288286602/1677261996355#chp1.

49. Cornell, "Processes of Native Nationhood: The Indigenous Politics of Self-Government": 7.

50. "Archived—An Act to Amend and Continue the Act 32 and 33 Victoria, Chapter 3; and to Establish and Provide for the Government of the Province

of Manitoba, S.C. 1870, c. 3," Legislation and Regulations, Indigenous Services Canada, last modified September 15, 2010, https://www.sac-isc.gc.ca/eng/1100 100010208/1618941272137.

51. Paul Chartrand, "Aboriginal Rights: The Dispossession of the Métis," *Osgoode Hall Law Journal* 29, no. 3 (December 31, 1991), https://www .semanticscholar.org/paper/Aboriginal-Rights%3A-The-Dispossession-of-the -M%C3%A9tis-Chartrand/oeb1a097d909451f70e11a0463504cf8d6776de7.

52. See Frank Tough, *'As Their Natural Resources Fail': Native Peoples and the Economic History of Northern Manitoba, 1870–1930,* (Vancouver: UBC Press, 1996), Appendix 1.

53. Darren O'Toole, "Manitoba Métis Federation Inc. v. Canada: Breathing New Life into the 'Empty Box' Doctrine of 'Indian Title,'" *Alberta Law Review* 52, no. 3 (2015): 674.

54. After highlighting the unilateral nature of the Manitoba Act as distinct from treaty-based agreements, it is crucial to clarify that this analysis does not presume the Canadian state regarded Indigenous nations engaged in treaty-making as equals or sovereign counterparts in a manner similar to its own nationhood. Instead, we aim to expose the discrepancy between the theoretical framework of nation-to-nation treaties and the practical subordination of Indigenous Peoples under settler colonialism, which the Manitoba Act exemplifies by its unilateral approach. We argue that this distinctively alienated the Métis and diminished their claims to nationhood and sovereignty.

55. To be sure, this injustice has since been deployed by Métis nationalists as an example of the historical injury used to ground their claims to nationhood today. But this possesses far less transformative potential than a treaty would have. See Bart Bonikowski, "Ethno-Nationalist Populism and the Mobilization of Collective Resentment," *British Journal of Sociology* 68, S1 (2017): S181–S213; and Eugen Weber, "Nationalism and the Politics of Resentment." *The American Scholar* 63, no. 3 (1994): 421–28 for discussions on the role that resentment and perceived injury play in nationalist foment.

56. *Daniels v. Canada (Indian Affairs and Northern Development),* 2016 SCC 12, (2016] 1 S.C.R. 99; *Manitoba Métis Federation Inc. v. Canada (Attorney General),* 2013 SCC 14, (2013] 1 S.C.R. 623.

57. See Adam Gaudry, "New Métis," Métis Identity Appropriation, and the Displacement of Living Métis Culture," *American Indian Quarterly* 42, no. 2 (2018): 162–90; Darryl Leroux, *White Claims to Indigenous Identity* (Winnipeg: University of Manitoba Press, 2019); Jessica Kolopenuk, "The Pretendian Problem," *Canadian Journal of Political Science* 56, no. 2 (June, 2023): 468–73; Adam Gaudry and Chris Andersen, "Daniels v. Canada: Racialized Legacies, Settler Self-Indigenization and the Denial of Indigenous Peoplehood," *TOPIA: Canadian Journal of Cultural Studies* 36 (2016): 19–30.

58. John Ralston Saul, *A Fair Country: Telling Truths About Canada,* Reprint ed. (Toronto: Penguin Canada, 2009), 3.

59. Nadasdy, "Boundaries among Kin."

ITSIIPOOTSIKIMSKAI[1]

SANDRA BARTLETT ATWOOD, NINNA PIIKSII (CHIEF BIRD) MIKE BRUISED HEAD,
MARK W. BRUNSON, AAHSAOPI (STATE OF BEING) LAVERNE FIRST RIDER, TIM FRANDY,
JAMES MAFFIE, AAKAOMO'TSSTAKI (MANY VICTORIES) MICHELLE PROVOST,
and MIINIIPOKAA (BERRY CHILD) PETER WEASEL MOCCASIN

Complementary Worldviews Aligning: A Relational Approach to STEM Education

Abstract

Educators in Canada face federal and provincial mandates arising from the TRC Calls to Action (2012) to incorporate First Nations, Métis, and Inuit (FNMI) perspectives across the curriculum. Yet it is not uncommon to hear K–12 educators as well as some university faculty asking, "How do I incorporate Indigenous culture into science? Is it even possible?" This paper not only describes how it is possible but also explains why it is necessary, providing a theoretical framework and practical examples of how Western approaches to science, technology, engineering, and math (STEM) knowledge can be braided with Indigenous treatments of these knowledge categories and disciplines. Historically, Niitsitapi (Blackfoot) and other Indigenous worldviews have been systematically and systemically dismissed by the sciences and primarily confined to the humanities. Therefore, to move beyond merely learning *about* Indigenous cultures and lean into learning *from* them (i.e., learn through the lens of Indigenous cultures), we must (1) teach Niitsitapi and other Indigenous stories beyond the humanities classroom; (2) better engage the etiological, ontological, epistemological, axiological, and practical traditions of Niitsitapi and other Indigenous Peoples; and (3) operationalize pedagogical and methodological models that acknowledge, respect, and embody Indigenous ways of knowing and being in STEM education.

FOR CENTURIES, Indigenous ways of knowing and being (IWKB) have been dismissed, if not suppressed, by Western science (Battiste 2013; Burkhart 2019b; Cajete 1994, 2000; Chambers and Gillespie 2000; Kimmerer 2013; Little Bear 2000, 2011, 2015, 2016; Smith 2012; Lindstrom et al. 2021; Wilson 2008). With the "European Enlightenment" came the idea that spirituality and "supernatural" phenomenon could not be investigated by scientific methods (Hanohano 1999; Strevens 2020). Consequently, Western science and religion (and with it, spirituality) were deemed mutually incompatible and eventually became regarded as epistemologically distinct domains with science being seen as the more accurate and reliable of the two. Colonial expansion spread this Eurocentric worldview and episteme abroad contributing to hegemonic agendas to not only assimilate Indigenous peoples and eradicate Indigenous knowledge systems, languages, and practices but also, in many cases, eliminate Indigenous Peoples altogether. After decades and for some Indigenous groups, centuries of subjugation, a tipping point came in 1999 with Section 35 of the *Declaration on Science and the Uses of Scientific Knowledge* (2000) which states, "Modern science does not constitute the only form of knowledge, and closer links need to be established between this and other forms, systems and approaches to knowledge, for their *mutual enrichment and benefit*" (UNESCO and ICSU World Conference on Science 2000–; emphasis added). Section 36 elaborates:

> Traditional societies, many of them with strong cultural roots, have nurtured and refined systems of knowledge of their own, relating to such diverse domains as astronomy, meteorology, geology, ecology, botany, agriculture, physiology, psychology and health. Such knowledge systems represent an enormous wealth. Not only do *they harbor information as yet unknown to modern science,* but they are also expressions of other ways of living in the world, other relationships between society and nature, and other approaches to the acquisition and construction of knowledge. Special action must be taken to conserve and cultivate this fragile and diverse world heritage, in the face of globalization and the growing dominance of a single view of the natural world as espoused by science. *A closer linkage between science and other knowledge systems is expected to bring important advantages to both sides.*" (UNESCO and ICSU World Conference on Science 2000–; emphasis added)

Our essay responds to this appeal to establish closer links between Western science and Indigenous knowledge systems (including nonhuman peoples' "knowledge" systems or vantage points/stories) and explores some of the advantages of both sides.

We begin with a literature review of Indigenizing STEM. We then describe one author's methods for collaborating with Indigenous community partners to contextualize and address the problem with education that they are concerned about and set out to work on together. Following this, we share the results of our collaborative effort to develop a theoretical framework and practical examples for decolonizing and Indigenizing STEM in elementary, secondary, and postsecondary education by sharing what this looked like in Atwood's grade 3, 5, and college classrooms. We conclude this paper with a discussion that generalizes Atwood's lived experience applying the Elders' teachings to her STEM instruction for others who may wish to apply these methods to their own practice.

While many scholars, tribes, institutions, and agencies are talking about Indigenizing STEM with a focus on increasing Indigenous representation in STEM disciplines and fields (Conference Board of Canada n.d.; Stantec 2022; Stewart 2023), it is also critical to address the underrepresentation of Indigenous worldviews in STEM, in addition to the underrepresentation of Indigenous people pursuing STEM degrees and working in STEM fields (Battiste 2013; Battiste et al. 2002; Cajete 2000; Chambers and Gillespie 2000; Deloria 2004; LaDuke 1996; Little Bear 2000, 2011, 2015, 2016; Lydia Jennings [Wixárika & Yoeme Soil Scientist] pers. comm. August 31, 2021; Murray (pers. comm., March 10, 2022); Ranalda L. Tsosie [Diné chemist] pers. comm., April 4, 2022; Stewart 2007, 2023). Gaudry and Lorenz (2018) draw attention specifically to the way "Canadian universities and colleges have felt pressured to [I]ndigenize their institutions. What '[I]indigenization' has looked like, however, has varied significantly" (218). After surveying twenty-five Indigenous academics and their allies, they developed a three-part spectrum for differentiating what Indigenization means, with *Indigenous inclusion* on one end, *reconciliation Indigenization* in the middle, and *decolonial Indigenization* on the other end. "Conceptually, [I]ndigenization represents a move to expand the academy's still-narrow conceptions of knowledge, to include Indigenous perspectives in transformative ways" (218). They conclude, "that despite using reconciliatory language, post-secondary institutions in Canada focus predominantly on Indigenous inclusion" (218) (i.e., increasing the number of Indigenous bodies in the academy without changing the structure of the academy).

Some postcolonial scholars (Dotson 2011; Fricker 2007; Nadasdy 1999; Spivak 1988) have approached the historical (if not general) disregard for Indigenous ontologies and epistemologies in terms of "epistemic violence [and] practices of silencing" (Dotson 2011, 236). Fricker (2007) contends that epistemic justice goes beyond making information and education available to marginalized groups. She maintains that to understand epistemic justice we must consider what epistemic *injustice* is, suggesting that epistemic injustice involves being wronged expressly in one's capacity as a knower. She classifies such injustices into two categories, testimonial and hermeneutical injustice:

> Testimonial injustice occurs when prejudice causes a hearer to give a deflated level of credibility to a speaker's word. Hermeneutical injustice occurs at a prior stage, when a gap in collective interpretive resources puts someone at an unfair disadvantage when it comes to making sense of their social[-environmental] experiences. (Fricker 2007, 1)

An example of the first might be a scientist not taking someone seriously because they don't have a Western degree or because their knowledge of the world is based in creation stories and relationships with seemingly inanimate "objects" and phenomenon; an example of the second might be suffering from a sense of incoherence and spiritual disconnection from having to navigate a culture that lacks the critical concept of comprehensive relational animacy. Fricker (2007, 1) speaks of the first being caused by "prejudice in the economy of credibility and the second by structuralist prejudice in the economy of collective hermeneutical resources." Burkhart (2019a) further explores the sources of epistemic violence and the problem with a single privileged or dominant explanation for how the world exists, contending that knowledge systems

> where land is a living, breathing relative and the continual creative source of life, thinking, knowing, feeling, and being . . . [can actually trigger] the operations of epistemic guardianship within the settler colonial epistemologies . . . [which] hold up and justify the false [or at least incomplete] worlds of white supremacy and Euro-supremacy . . . This delusional [or limited] epistemic world serves settler colonial power because *it presents the imaginary [or incomplete] world of Euro-supremacy as the entire world.* Settler colonialism, then, is not any particular historical event or set of historical events but rather a structure, as articulated in Patrick Wolfe's work—a structure of power that produces subjugating effects in a myriad of ways, including the subjugation of the production and recognition of Indigenous knowledge. (Burkhart 2019a, 2; emphasis added)

When Indigenous worldviews are solicited or welcomed by science, the focus is most often on ecosystem, medicinal, and climate knowledge (Ninna Piiksii/Bruised Head, oral teaching, November 22, 2021). Traditional knowledges are seen as having relevant contributions to make to these fields in terms of millennia of observations and experiences with the natural world. However, traditional knowledge (TK), Indigenous knowledge (IK), or Indigenous ways of knowing and being (IWKB) often get decontextualized and generalized in the process and the more profound contributions of Indigenous knowing go unnoticed or intentionally ignored. For example, some scientists will accommodate things like plants and animals being agentive but aren't interested in Indigenous understandings and experiences of entities such as rocks, water, words, numbers, energies, and subatomic particles, also being alive, sentient, and interrelated to each other and humans. In Blackfoot Elders and scholars Betty Bastien and Duane Mistaken Chief's (2004) book *Blackfoot Ways of Knowing*[2] they explain that Blackfoot epistemology and "sacred science" (3) "begin with sacred knowledge held in the stories and ceremonies that have been handed down through a web of kinship alliances . . . [and that] Ihtsipaitapiiyo'pa (the Source of Life) is the great mystery that is in everything in the universe" (77). They elaborate that

> spiritual energies permeate the cosmic universe from Ihtsipaitapiiyo'pa (the Source of Life). These energies manifest in physical form, and from them Niitapaissao'pi (the nature of being) is created. Based on this ontological view, we can establish how knowledge is understood and what the process of Kakyosin (coming to know) is. The process of knowing is based on the interrelationships of natural alliances. Knowledge is generated through these relationships. Spiritual energies are the ultimate substance of the universe from which all life forms originate (Ihtsipaitapiiyo'pa), including knowledge [herself]. (Bastien and Mistaken Chief 2007, 3–4)

Classical Western approaches to science are often reductionary, linear, and objective. A problem is observed through a zoomed-in lens (often a literal microscope), a hypothesis is developed, and experiments are carried out with the intent to falsify the hypothesis. If the results support the hypothesis, the new theory is embraced (often without any immediate concern for how the specific theory relates to a general theory or the whole) until a more reliable understanding can be procured through future developments. In this way, Western thinking is continually moving from an older understanding toward a newer, presumably more accurate understanding or knowledge of the world. By contrast, as explained by Blackfoot colleague John Chief Calf (pers. comm. November 2018), the Blackfoot approach to a problem is holistic, cyclic, and relational. Relationships with nonhuman relatives of whom nature is comprised guide the discovery process rather than individual intellect or preconceived theories. Problems are observed from the wide-angle lens of Eagle as he soars above Earth. From this vantage point, the past, present, and future can be viewed at once and patterns emerge. In this essay we submit that Indigenous science is informed by relationships with Níksókowaawáiks ("all my relatives") and the stories they give, and that a genuine and nonhierarchical consideration of Western STEM subjects through the ontological and epistemological lenses of Indigenous Peoples will produce new and important insights for describing complex systems and solving complex problems or "wicked problems" as coined by Rittel and Webber (1973).

Methodology

For this study, we paired the collective method (Itsiipootsikimskai 2023) with coproduction (Meadow et al. 2015) to identify, define, and begin to solve a problem that Niitsitapi or Blackfoot community partners cared about and wanted to work on together. The collective method is a research method that allows investigators to ground their work in the axiomatic foundational Indigenous understanding that everything in the world is alive and interrelated. The method not only allows for intuition and spiritual analysis of relational storied data but requires it. We engaged with this method of inquiry for discovery purposes, but the method is also the essence of Niitsitapi science, which we used to decolonize and Indigenize Western STEM subjects/disciplines and pedagogies (see table 1). We address this further in the "results" section of this article. From 2019 to present Atwood spent over nine hundred hours learning from Niitsitapi Elders, scholars, and community members as she participated in a master of education program primarily taught by Elders using Blackfoot methods and pedagogies, on the land, in the classroom, in ceremony, and many ongoing one-on-one conversations. During that time, Atwood received permission to document some of the Elders' teachings and conversations with the intent that she should embody the knowledge and share it in a good way. As coinvestigators and coauthors, Elders have guided the collection and interpretation of their story data as well as the distribution of the results of this study.

Coproduction allows researchers to begin research without specific questions or problems in mind (Armitage et al. 2011; Latulippe and Klenk 2020; Meadow et al. 2015). The method is grounded in relationship building and listening. It seeks to observe how community partners frame an issue and to understand the terms and knowledge systems they use to interpret an issue (Meadow et al. 2015). As a problem emerges, researchers bring their skills and knowledge to the table and allow the community to guide the research and put those skills and knowledge to use to facilitate positive change together for the benefit of the host community and society as a whole (Latulippe and Klenk 2020). Latulippe and Klenk (2020) emphasize the importance of not only "making room" for Indigenous partners and their perspectives and practices but also *moving over*. In some cases, knowledge is shared by the community while the researcher primarily observes and listens; at other times knowledge is coproduced by generating new synthetic knowledge or braiding Western and Indigenous knowledges together (Armitage et al. 2011). Some issues that came up repeatedly in our conversations included: (1) the way IK or IWKB are not taken seriously by the sciences/scientists and are often confined to the humanities; (2) the lack of engagement by educators and scholars to understand the fundamental differences between Indigenous and Western ways of knowing and being; and (3) the lack of Indigenous perspectives and methods in curricula and pedagogies, particularly in the sciences.

Table 1. Indigenous Collective Methods in Relation to Quantitative and Qualitative Analytical Frameworks

METHOD/ METHODOLOGY	QUANTITATIVE	QUALITATIVE	NIITSITAPI/COLLECTIVE
ONTOLOGICAL ORIENTATION	Animate vs. inanimate	Animate vs. inanimate	Comprehensive relational animacy
EPISTEMIC ORIENTATION	Deductive (aims to test existing theories)	Inductive (aims to develop theories)	Axiomative (aims to extend and embody foundational truths/stories)
	Scientific method	Comparative, evaluative, phenomenological, interview, and grounded theory methods	Axiomatic, experiential, and conversational methods
	Falsification	Interpretation	Interrelation
	Reductive	Constructive	Generative/creative and holistic
	Top-down (linear)	Bottom-up (linear)	Inside-out and outside-in (cyclic)
	Objective	Subjective (constructivism allows limited intersubjectivity)	Intersubjective
	Closed-ended questions	Open-ended questions	Energy exchange, alignment, ceremony
	Experimental	Conversational	Experiential and relational
	Mathematical and statistical analyses	Perceptual and contextual analyses	Spiritual/intuitional analysis
	Observation using 5 senses	Observation using 5 senses	Observation using 6 senses (Spirit)
	Involves theoretical and empirical knowledge	Involves empirical and theoretical knowledge	Involves spiritual, embodied, and dream knowledge
	Measurable, quantifiable data	Categorical, approximative data	Relational, storied data

To address educators and scholars' lack of engagement with and under-standing of worldview differences, Atwood simultaneously conducted semi-structured interviews and conversations with over two hundred elementary, secondary, and postsecondary educators as they met in various profes-sional development meetings, staff lunchrooms, classrooms, and social media chat groups regarding the decolonial Indigenization of curricula and pedagogy. As she became more knowledgeable about local Niitsitapi perspectives and pedagogies, and with the encouragement of Blackfoot Elders and mentors, she began to address concerns 1 and 3 by creating spaces for IWKB in her own practice, which over time consisted of a grade-five science class, a grade-three class where she taught all subjects, and a community college "Introduction to Indigenous Studies" course. Following her ethnographic and participatory action research with these two study groups (i.e., the Niitsitapi community and the teaching community in southern Alberta, which lies in the heart of Niitsitapi traditional territory), she used her own teaching practice in the classroom, professional development presentations, and conference presentations to explore the application of IWKB to science curricula and pedagogy. To address Niitsitapi partners' concerns as well as educator partners' questions (e.g., How do I incorporate Indigenous culture into science? Is it even possible?), we developed a theoretical framework for decolonial Indigenization of standard Western curriculum and pedagogy in ways that permit and foster greater equity and inclusion of diverse ways of knowing and being across the curriculum. Phenomenological research of this sort is becoming an increasingly prominent part of the scholarly traditions of education and geography as phenomenological approaches tend to align with and make room for IWKB, allowing for greater complementarity when collaborating with Indigenous research partners and braiding Western and Indigenous research methods and knowledges. In education, "Phenomenology has been used primarily as a methodological approach to illuminate lived experience . . . it has also occasionally provided possibilities for articulating theories of teaching and learning in close relation with concrete practice" (Brinkmann and Friesen 2018, 591), for example, SoTL (the science of teaching and learning) research.

Many educators find it relatively easy to incorporate IWKB into social studies, language arts, music, art, and even fitness-wellness subjects but find it to be more challenging with STEM subjects. From a Western perspective, IWKB appear to have three epistemologically distinct or noninterrelated components: observation, stories from the Elders, and a spiritual or revelatory process of some kind. Many science scholars and educators then conclude that only observation can be considered valid because it is the only component that aligns with Western scientific methods. The other two components of Indigenous knowing are left to the humanities and social sciences to consider. However, for Niitsitapi, their words for knowing, like *Kakyosin*, necessarily include all three of these elements, and one doesn't actually know something until they have been observant of their surroundings, learned the stories of the nonhuman relatives they are observing—and with whom they have aligned themselves in relationships leading to "thinking like a tree" or a river or a rock and so on—knowing the vantage point and positionality of those relatives. For these reasons, in our study we focused on reimagining STEM subjects; however, the reality is that IWKB are holistic. There are no distinctions between what Western education considers individual subjects or disciplines. As such, the methods for understanding any "subject" are the same: observation, listening, relationship (being on and with the land experiencing the spiritual connection with "all my relatives" and caring for them like you would a small child, respecting them as ancestors and Elders); and renewal (prayer, ceremony). Bastien and Mistaken Chief (2004) describe it this way, "This knowledge is alive" (5); they further explain:

> Knowing results from being aware, observant, and reflective. Kakyosin creates and reveals the living knowledge of a cosmic universe. It is living because it is generated from the relationships among the knowledge from Ihtsipaitapiiyo'pa, Akaitapiwa, the cosmic universe, *and myself*. The knowledge exists as long as the relationships with the alliances continue and changes as these relationships change. Knowledge that is generated from these relationships can only be understood and acquired through living and communicating with the natural and cosmic alliances. As a result, the understanding of the knowledge and wisdom that Kaaahsinnooniksi [grandparents or Elders] transferred to me through Nitaisstammatsokoyi ("what I have been shown or instructed") is only achieved through my experiences; the depth of my own knowledge is relative to understanding my place and responsibility among the alliances. (5—emphasis added) . . . This way of knowing is of a different nature than the knowledge generated using cross-cultural or alien perspectives developed by Eurocentred sciences. (Bastien and Mistaken Chief 2004, 1)

Allan et al. (2018) also acknowledge the importance of these emotional and holistic aspects of Indigenizing education:

> Indigenization requires that equitable space for Indigenous knowledges and perspectives be held and explored in the classroom. Many institutions have defined Indigenization on the basis of current, authentic relationships, and there are nuances and different approaches to Indigenization. What a teacher needs to be mindful of is that Indigenizing one's practice is an emotional journey as well as an intellectual examination of how systems of knowledge can complement and coexist in any field of study.

The declaration by the UNESCO and ICSU World Conference on Science (2000) maintains the importance of learning from Indigenous knowledge systems for the mutual benefit of Westerners and Indigenous Peoples. In *The Metaphysics of Modern Existence*, Deloria (1977) explains why Indigenizing the sciences is so critical for Indigenous learners: "No matter how well educated an Indian may become, he or she always suspects that Western culture is not an adequate representation of reality. Life therefore becomes a schizophrenic balancing act wherein one holds that the creation, migration, and ceremonial stories of the tribe are true and that the Western European view of the world is also true" (viii). The theoretical framework we have developed in this essay addresses this problem by making epistemological space for students to make their own relational meanings while learning and applying Western science, technology, engineering, and mathematics.

We also employed library (including educational and historical) research to further contextualize, respond to, and corroborate the ethnographic or story data shared by Blackfoot and educator partners and to inform the coproduction of the theoretical framework, pedagogy, and examples we developed.

Results

"Some other tribes [and non-Indigenous people] think of 'supernatural' beings but not the Blackfoot. Everything is reality, it's science, it's objective [not mysterious], we see the world as it is. Our ways are based in science, not just faith. The Societies guard this science. There is science behind the supernatural" (Blackfoot Elder, Aahsaopi [State of Being]/Laverne First Rider, pers. comm., April 4, 2021).

Decolonial Theoretical Framework

Blackfoot Elder, Ninna Piiksii (Chief Bird)/Mike Bruised Head (oral teaching, October 12, 2019) shared that all teaching begins with creation stories, pitsistoyi (from the outset).[3] When teaching about Niitsitapi culture or any other topic, including STEM, every teaching is grounded in foundational stories. He also instructed that in Niitsitapi pedagogy one should then situate themselves within those stories by sharing their own story niinohkanistssksinipi (this is the way I know it [the world or reality] to be; speaking personally).[4] This became a guiding principle for developing a decolonial theoretical framework and pedagogy.

Because Niitsitapi worldview and pedagogy are holistic and grounded in interpersonal relationship with nature (spomitapiiksi, above or sky beings/persons; ksahkomitapiiksi, earth beings/persons; soyiitapiiksi, water beings/persons), the framework we developed is cross-curricular/interdisciplinary and each worldview (Indigenous and Western) is presented non-hierarchically (i.e., not arranged according to level of importance, on an equal footing). The framework (which in its essence entails creating space in the curriculum for things in nature to be alive, interrelated, and aligned with each other and humans), exemplified in the following figures by a concept wall, is a result of the research Atwood conducted among Niitsitapi and educator communities. It addresses their concerns and questions with regard to the decolonial Indigenization of STEM education as well as the federal and provincial mandates requiring educators to incorporate FNMI foundational knowledge into the curriculum and the appeal of the UNESCO and ICSU World Conference on Science to establish closer links between Western science and other knowledge systems. In this application of the framework, Atwood started with the concepts of "perspective" and "worldview," along with an overarching question that honors the way Niitsitapi Elders talk about all knowledge deriving from relationship with land: "How might diverse world perspectives help us describe and solve complex social, economic, and environmental problems?" Perspective is also a grade-three science and art concept, so it allowed Atwood to present that concept in more holistic and connected ways. Conceptual learning is effective because it allows students to create a big "file folder" in their minds in which they can store related facts rather than creating new "folders" for each isolated fact they learn. Once students understand a concept, knowledge transfer becomes easier, and they can creatively use old knowledge to solve new problems as they make connections and see relationships between concepts.

Atwood then extracted all the main concepts from the grade-three curriculum and put them down the Y axis and put Kainai/Blackfoot (Indigenous) and Canadian (Western) worldviews across the X axis and designed the wall-sized graph. She began with Blackfoot origin stories and perspectives to present an alternate worldview by which to compare Western knowledge. In this way, Western knowledge becomes one way of knowing, rather than the primary, only, or most valid way. Naturally things like "rocks" show up in multiple concepts from origin stories to wayfinding to structures as they are among the oldest relatives and have the most stories.

Here is an example of one grade-three objective "time" and how rich that concept becomes when considered across cultures. For example, some Blackfoot sacred rock cairn circles, such as the one in Bighorn, Montana, are known to accurately align with the annual heliacal rising of celestial beings like Sirius, Aldebaran, and Rigel when they first become visible on the eastern horizon. Atwood also talks about how Indigenous and Western cultures celebrate New Year at a different time, as each culture has their own reasons for when the new year begins. Similarly, wayfinding gets complicated as students compare and contrast Western curriculum objectives on map reading and cardinal directions with Indigenous Peoples' notions about the four directions. Additionally, many IWKB privilege east rather than north as the primary coordinate. Boroditsky's (2017) research on how language shapes the way we think allows for conversation about how knowledge is embedded

FIGURES 1 AND 2. A partial recreation of the overarching question and concepts from Atwood's grade-three concept wall. Photo by Sandra Bartlett Atwood.

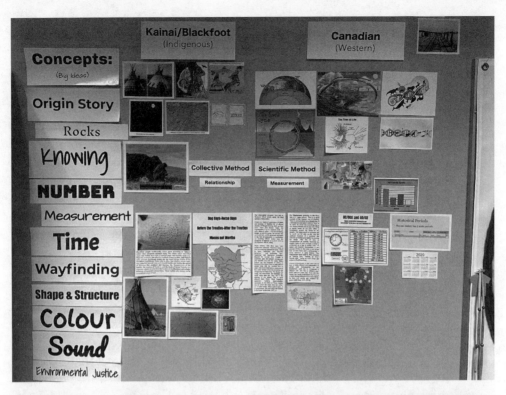

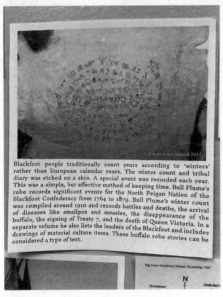

Blackfoot people traditionally count years according to 'winters' rather than European calendar years. The winter count and tribal diary was etched on a skin. A special event was recorded each year. This was a simple, but effective method of keeping time. Bull Plume's robe records significant events for the North Peigan Nation of the Blackfoot Confederacy from 1764 to 1879. Bull Plume's winter count was compiled around 1910 and records battles and deaths, the arrival of diseases like smallpox and measles, the disappearance of the buffalo, the signing of Treaty 7, and the death of Queen Victoria. In a separate volume he also lists the leaders of the Blackfoot and includes drawings of material culture items. These buffalo robe stories can be considered a type of text.

For Aboriginal peoples, time just is. Benjamin Whorf writing about the Hopi concept of time states:

(Time) is a realm of expectancy, of desire and purpose, of vitalizing life, of efficient causes, of thought thinking itself out from inner realm (the Hopian heart) into manifestation. It is in a dynamic state, yet not a state of motion – It is not advancing toward us out of a future, but already with us in vital form, and its dynamism is at work in the field of eventuating or manifesting, i.e. evolving without motion from the subjective by degrees to a result which is the objective. (Whorf, 1950).

Plains Indians, Little Bear says, have similar time concepts. "Blackfoot thinks of time on a two-day operational sense. There is 'now,' 'tomorrow,' and 'day-after tomorrow.' And backwards, 'now,' 'yesterday,' and 'day-before yesterday.' Beyond the two-day limit, forward or backward, past and present amalgamate and become one and the same. Plains Indians are not incapable of talking or thinking of the distant future or past, but it is always done with the 'constant flux' in mind. One of the implications arising out of this notion of time is that the ancestors are always only two days away. The stories, the songs, the ceremonies, the teachings are never more than two days old in the memory of the people. This is quite different from Pierre Elliott Trudeau's statement, typifying Euro-Canadian worldview, to the effect of "these treaties are not worth the paper they are written on." In other words, what is past is past...it is gone forever. The only thing that matters is the future." (Little Bear, 2001, 5)

For Westerners, according to Little Bear, time is a major referent. Time is a good example of the Western way of thinking. "Time is conceptualized as a straight line. If a [Westerner] attempted to picture "time" in his mind, he would see something like a river flowing toward and on past him. What is behind would be the past. What is immediately around him would be the present. The future would be upstream, but he would not be able to see very far upstream because of a waterfall, the waterfall symbolizing the barrier to knowing the future. This line of time is conceptualized as quantity especially as lengths made of units. A length of time is envisioned as a row of similar units." "A logical and inherent characteristic of the concept of time is that once a unit of the river of time flows past a [Westerner] it never returns-it is gone forever. This characteristic lends itself to other concepts as "wasting time," "making up time," "buying time," "being on time" which are unique to the [Westerner].

Another characteristic is that each unit of time is totally different and independent of similar units. Consequently, for the [Westerner], each day is considered a different unit, and thus a different day; every year is a new year. From this the reader can readily understand why there is a need among [Westerners] to have names for days and months and numbers for years. (Little Bear, 1975, 337-8).

FIGURES 3, 4, AND 5. Partial re-creation of some of the concepts mentioned in the text: for example, origin stories, rocks, knowing, number, and time. The artifacts under each category are meant to be visual representations of stories and content taught throughout the year, a visual reminder of the universality and diversity of meanings for each concept. Photo by Sandra Bartlett Atwood.

in and shaped by languages. She describes how the Kuuk Thaayorre people of Pormpuraaw, on the western edge of York, Australia, use cardinal directions for everything *except* wayfinding, as they are continuously aware of their spatial location and direction. For example, if you wanted to tell someone they had an ant on their left leg, you would say, "You have an ant on your southwest leg." To say "hello," you would say, "Which way are you going?" to which one would report their heading, "North-northeast and the far distance." Perhaps most interesting for the comparative purposes of Atwood's class, for the Kuuk Thaayorre, time doesn't get locked onto the body but rather onto the landscape. For example, when given a series of pictures of the same person as a baby, child, teen, adult, and an elderly person, they didn't arrange the pictures from left to right the way Westerners typically do unless they were facing south. However, when they were facing north, they organized the pictures from right to left. When they sat facing west, the pictures were lined up moving away from the body. When facing east, they arranged the pictures coming toward the body. These are just a few examples of how a worldview approach can enrich and decolonize STEM concepts.

Considering Ninna Piiksii/Mike Bruised Head's teachings that all learning and knowledge production begins with creation stories, Atwood put that concept first, which allowed students to compare and contrast the origin stories of Blackfoot (and other Indigenous Peoples) with the "creation stories" of Western science (e.g., rock and water cycles, big bang, and the evolution of species). Origin stories help students imagine the world through the eyes of other peoples. For example, many Indigenous stories speak of everything coming into existence by thought or sound vibrations (students often make connections with the physics unit on sound energy as they reason through the possible compatibility of Indigenous and Western accounts of sound vibrations). Niitsitapi origin stories necessarily begin with Ihtsipaitapiiyo'pa (The Essence or Source of Life). Bastien and Mistaken Chief (2004) explain how this knowledge relates to what Western science calls natural laws:

> Ihtsipaitapiiyo'pa—Sacred power, spirit or force that links concepts; life force; term used when addressing the sacred power and the cosmic universe; Source of Life; sun as manifestation of the Source of Life; great mystery; together with Niitpaitapiiyssin [life or lifeworld] identifies the meaning and purpose of life. Ihtsipaitapiiyo'pa is that which causes or allows us to live. The term "natural law" does not have a direct Siksikaitsitapiwahsin [Blackfoot word] equivalent; however, it is through Ihtsipaitapiiyopa that all "natural laws" are governed. It is Ihtsipaitapiiyopaa that orchestrates the universe. Its laws govern the universe including human life. (Bastien and Mistaken Chief 2004, 200)

By leading with Niitsitapi or Blackfoot worldview (specifically Kainai, one of the four tribes of the Blackfoot Confederacy), all students understand that one way the world exists is that everything in nature is alive and interrelated to each other and humans in nonhierarchical ways. Then as they move into learning the Western STEM content for the rest of the year, students can think about how Western science, technology, engineering, and math might be informed by comprehensive relational animacy, and students can make their own meaning of how the world exists. Atwood has also done this in reverse, weaving in the sciences while teaching college-level Indigenous studies courses to Euro-settler, Indigenous, and international students who are earning degrees in nursing, education, criminal justice, agriculture, social work, and environmental science. One Blackfoot student from the college course provided this feedback, which seems to indicate the effectiveness of the framework and pedagogy, "You're the perfect person to teach this course because you understand my people and you understand your people and you know how to make your people understand my people." A local student who had attended K–12 schools where many Blackfoot students were enrolled also reflected about how Atwood's approach was different:

> As we discuss the effects of Western colonization, I reflect on my Indigenous classmates over the years [and how it must have felt for them to live in two worlds]. Knowing more truth of [their ways of knowing and being] brings it close to home knowing how this must be affecting people close to me. . . . I have noticed a change in the Indigenous students in our class. They seem more willing to speak up and tell us their [perspectives], a noticeable difference from other past classes, giving the rest of us a more in-depth understanding [of their knowledge]. Hearing first-hand accounts from the students around me and the emotional response they have makes you flip the script and look at Western colonization [and worldview] as nothing short of domineering and incomplete. (oral teaching, April 12, 2023)

Each of the following STEM subheadings in this section include story data from Niitsitapi Elders and other Indigenous Peoples that illustrate Niitsitapi and other Indigenous perspectives on science, technology, and math respectively; historical data representing overlapping perspectives of various Western scientists; and vignettes of Atwood's experiences applying the decolonial Indigenized framework in her own teaching practice.

Relational Science
While Atwood was teaching the chemical formula for water (H_2O) to a grade-five class, one Blackfoot student exclaimed:

Oh, I get it now, hydrogen and oxygen are our relatives, and they must have made an alliance so we can have water, it's hard to break the hydrogen and oxygen apart now because the relatives honor their alliances. They don't break their promises, it's their responsibility to be water. They agreed to do that for all the other relatives who need water to live and grow. (oral teaching, February 13, 2018)

The only thing Atwood had done to Indigenize the course was apply the theoretical framework by discussing on the first day of class that for many Indigenous Peoples, nature is alive and interrelated. This simple opening gave Blackfoot students permission to think like a water molecule and make meaning of Western knowledge in a way that was consistent with their own ways of knowing. Interestingly, Henry Eyring, a renowned physical chemist, "often talked about 'living' among molecules . . . getting acquainted with the molecules as if they were your friends and knowing what their nature is and what they will do . . . [stating that] [u]nless [a chemist] just gets lost in his work and feels that knowing molecules is like knowing people, he probably won't get far" (Eyring 2008, 193–95). This method of imagining oneself, or as the Elders would say, *aligning* oneself with atomic particles is similar to Albert Einstein's imagining/aligning himself with a beam of light (i.e., discerning the vantage point of subatomic particles or light and thereby coming to know their stories). Einstein credits this activity and other "thought experiments" as he liked to call them, for lending critical insights to the development of his revolutionary theories of special and general relativity. The following statement by Tewa scholar Gregory Cajete (1994) suggests that scientists may have these experiences because all the relatives "are alive; and you must give them good talk" (102), implying that if we acknowledge, respect, and align ourselves with them, the relatives will gift us their knowledge—their stories. Non-Indigenous theoretical quantum physicist Jim Wheeler shared, "Space, unlike time, requires the existence of a multiplicity of conscious beings that trust one another" (pers. comm., September 4, 2010). And while he was merely sharing his scientific research on spacetime, his conclusions complement Indigenous understandings of relationality. Similarly, non-Indigenous mitochondrial biologist Martin Picard and behavioral neuroscientist Carmen Sandi (2021) in their paper "*The Social Nature of Mitochondria: Implications for Human Health*," describe the unexpected results of their study:

Sociality [relationality] has deep evolutionary roots and underlies biological complexity. Mitochondria exhibit social behavior . . . [they] are social organelles. The extension of social principles across levels of biological complexity is a theoretical shift that emphasizes the role of communication and interdependence in cell biology, physiology, and neuroscience. . . . A social mitochondria perspective impacts our understanding of human health and behavior. (Picard and Sandi 2021, 596)

When teaching the water cycle, Atwood teaches the Western science content but then to encourage a relational understanding of water's story and knowledge, she has students depict the water cycle in a story, tracking a particular entity of water throughout the cycle. One student told the story starting from "dinosaur pee," another imagining they were a cloud, aligning themselves to describe those final moments when they could no longer hold the moisture before letting it fall onto a mountain where a tired and sweaty hiker took his hat off and lifted his head to feel the rain on his face, and so on. Perhaps the most poignant and yet therapeutic example was a young Blackfoot student who, in one year, had lost each of her parents, then a beloved aunt, and finally her grandmother who was her legal guardian. The circumstances surrounding each loss and the resulting trauma had really impacted her. She chose to write about the tear that welled up in her eye until it spilled over her eyelashes onto her cheek the very moment they closed the lid of her mother's casket. She proceeded to depict a journey for that teardrop that was at times exciting and joyful and other times scary and dark until it finally evaporated into the sky one hot summer day, and the tear was happy to be closer to heaven for a while. Each of these students developed a relationship with water and water's story that day, which deepened their scientific understanding of the water cycle. Some of these students have since expressed that they can never forget the water cycle after that.

Relational Technology
Speaking on the history and evolution of modern science, Little Bear (2015) observes that science used to be principally about "delv[ing] into the unknown . . . stretching out there a bit, extending knowledge" whereas science today is defined and driven primarily by technology and what science can do. This shift away from science's "stronghold as the knowing enterprise that explains how the natural world works" (Dear 2006) has further alienated Native science. Many Indigenous Peoples worldwide have practices of offering tobacco, songs, chants, prayers to "raw materials" to gain permission from those relatives to use them for such diverse technologies as clothing, ornamentation, tools, weapons, lodging, pipes, surfboards, and food harvesting and preservation. Because most Indigenous Peoples consider things like water, fire, and rocks etc. to be alive and relatives, through alignment one can be in relationship with fire and come to think and act like fire. The Karuk tribe whose territory in what is now northern California have taken fire's story and used it to create a landscape that ensures they

have enough food, promoting their culture, health, and sovereignty while maintaining the spiritual and ecological balance of their homeland (Reed and Norgaard 2021). When Blackfoot people harvest a buffalo, it is not just for food. Traditionally they used every part of the buffalo out of respect for this relative who gives his life for their survival. Through relationship with buffalo, aligning themselves with this relative, and learning his stories, they were able to use this knowledge to develop many technologies. Today, the process is the same. In one method, a buffalo will step forward and offer itself, and the animal is taken with only one bullet. The animal is harvested on site within three hours to ensure the meat is good and the intestines, stomachs, etc. are usable. Even today, every part of the buffalo is "vowed" for. Nothing is wasted. This may be a feature of relational technology that could inform Western technology: nothing is discarded or seen as not having value or purpose. This often leads to a discussion about ethics and how different worldviews inform our ideas about technology, natural resources, and subsequently the ways we use them.

In another example, Ninna Piiksii/Mike Bruised Head (oral teaching, November 22, 2021) shared how after the Blackfoot were confined to reservations, they were given equipment and encouraged to be farmers: "Agriculture began the separation, changed the relationship with nature . . . the old people didn't want to touch that, 'We cannot cut the land, this is not right. Something's gonna come back on us, something's gonna disrupt the animals who live there and the chemicals, it's not good.' These are things we shouldn't mess with." Today, many of the technologies of the Blackfoot and other Indigenous Peoples are housed in museums in North America, Europe, and throughout the world. For Indigenous Peoples who consider these "artifacts" to be alive and relatives who gift their knowledge to humans, museums are seen as prisons that keep these "objects" from fulfilling their role in the community and their purpose for existing. For the Blackfoot, quillwork is a transferred rite. This involves ceremony to receive the rites to engage in relationship with all that encompasses the technology and art of quill work (National Museums Scotland 2022). Danielle Heavy Head elaborates,

> It is hard to express in English how important it is for Blackfoot people to connect with our historical items. To the Western perspective, these are just objects, but for the Blackfoot, they are living beings, and the museum visits are like being reunited with children who were taken away. Seeing and touching the items allows Blackfoot people to reconnect with the material and their ancestors. (As quoted in National Museums Scotland 2022)

Not having access to these items has hampered the ability for certain areas of knowledge to be awakened. Reactivating the objects (or technologies)

Every Part of the Buffalo Was Used

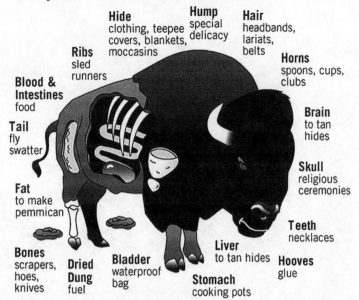

Hide
clothing, teepee covers, blankets, moccasins

Hump
special delicacy

Hair
headbands, lariats, belts

Ribs
sled runners

Horns
spoons, cups, clubs

Blood & Intestines
food

Brain
to tan hides

Tail
fly swatter

Skull
religious ceremonies

Fat
to make pemmican

Teeth
necklaces

Bones
scrapers, hoes, knives

Dried Dung
fuel

Bladder
waterproof bag

Liver
to tan hides

Hooves
glue

Stomach
cooking pots

FIGURE 6. From Phyllis A. Arnold and Betty Gibbs. *Canada Revisited 6*, 1E. © 1999 Nelson Education Ltd.

FIGURES 7 AND 8. Blackfeet Buffalo harvest, Heart Butte, MT, August 3, 2022. Photo by Sandra Bartlett Atwood.

FIGURE 9. Bison skulls waiting to be ground into glue and fertilizer circa 1870. Image is in the public domain.

creates a path to reconnect with Blackfoot knowledge and Blackfoot identity, which occurs through the spiritual connection within the alliances of kin and natural law (quoted in National Museums Scotland 2022).

There are many examples of diverse Indigenous Peoples who share similar beliefs and experiences of technologies *themselves* being imbued with spirit or spirits in one Mayan example. Boremanse (2000) examines the practice of "sacrifice" to the spirit of sewing machines that were brought into the community by anthropologists in the 1990s. Women interpreted the breaking of sewing machine needles while learning to sew as the machine "asking them for something." One of them said that if the "custom" had been performed, with respect to the machines, then such incidents would not have happened. After this, several women and men assembled and decided that the "custom" ought to be fulfilled. One said that performing the "custom" was a way of showing their gratitude to God for the machines. The Mayan folks of San Lucas believe sewing machines possess *x-kwiink.ul* (one of three categories of spirits, x-kwiink.ul is the spirit that inhabits "mundane" objects like houses, bridges, hammocks, tools, musical instruments, and so on). They believe that prayers made to each of the four cardinal directions, beginning with the east, and then feeding the machines will prevent them from harming the people with their needle. Harrison-Buck and Hendon (2018) explore similar accounts of relational technology in *Can Tools Have Souls? Maya Views of the Relations between Humans and Other-than-Human Persons.* There are also accounts of Blackfoot warriors having a relationship with their rifles. The rifles were cared for as more-than-objects and in turn the rifles gave enhanced accuracy, power, and protection to the shooter.

Relational Engineering

While engineering is technically a subcategory of technology—the branch of knowledge that deals with engineering and other applied sciences—we address engineering as a distinct category here because it is given that distinction in the STEM model. When teaching about bridges in grade three, Atwood encouraged her students to think like a river. She also combined the bridge unit with animal adaptations. They explored how various adaptations make animals well suited to their environments. They talked about what to consider to make a built structure suitable to its environment and considered various examples and nonexamples. They talked about Blackfoot understanding and experiences of relationship and alignment and how it helps them to think like an animal or a tree or a mountain, for example. One student asked, "Do Blackfoot people know how to think like a bridge? Maybe they could help me design my bridge." Some of their creative solutions to the final project of building the strongest or tallest or longest bridge they could out of simple materials were imaginative. In the oral presentation they made remarks such as, "If I could learn from spiders how they make their silk, I would use that for the cables on my bridge then it wouldn't matter how hard the wind blows, the bridge would just swing without breaking. I've seen that with spiderwebs, the wind blows hard but they don't break." Atwood discussed how some scientists and engineers call this method of designing structures patterned after nature, "biomimicry." She talks about *Kakyosin*, which is not only the Blackfoot word for "knowledge" and "knowing" but also refers to observing one's surroundings and aligning oneself with all the relatives. Bastien and Mistaken Chief (2004) elaborate on this type of biomimicry that is based in observations like engineers make but also relationship:

> The English terms 'to align' and 'to balance' refer to the Siksikaitsitapi [Blackfoot] understanding that there is an order of things or pattern that we can discern if we are observant (Kakyosin). We can see this in animal behaviour, weather cycles, etc. Through Kakyosin we align ourselves

with these patterns and are thus capable of achieving the same things the observed beings can. To give an exaggerated illustration: If we behave like a cat, think like a cat, etc., we eventually become cats. This is the idea behind alignment, alliances, and Kakyosin. We are adopting the order of things observed to such an extent that we may even become it. . . . Kakyosin isstaokakitsotsp [means] "Observation gives us intelligence knowledge and wisdom." (Bastien and Mistaken Chief 2004, 205–6)

Students explore examples of biomimicry that have been successful and others that have failed because engineers' observations of animals (and nature) weren't accurate, and from a Blackfoot perspective, they weren't aligned enough to understand the story the relatives were giving them. A local non-Indigenous construction engineer Pierre Bolduc unsuccessfully tried to build a dam on his property a few years ago. Then, he thought back to his youth, trapping beaver with his father and wondered if beavers might be able to help him. After observing some beavers and bringing to his property what seemed to be a family of five, he let them go to work. He had observed how beavers seemed to instinctively go to work building when they hear running water so he played the sounds of running water near the spot where he hoped they would build. He cut down trees and branches and put them in proximity to the spot where he wanted a dam, and the beavers did the rest. Bolduc humbly concluded, "It turns out we were the wrong kind of engineers to tackle this" (as quoted in May 2022).

In terms of relational science and its applications to engineering, the Blackfoot tipi is something Atwood studies with her classes. These tipis have a four-pole construction compared to the three-pole construction of most other Plains Tribes. This further stabilizes it to withstand the heavy gales of the local west winds. Recently there was a tipi that stayed standing while the Bow River flooded its banks, leaving a waterline halfway up the tipi covering. These tipis are often painted and considered to have a life of their own. "Blackfoot ways are embodied in Tipi . . . the whole universe is right there" (Ninna Piiksii/Bruised Head and Murray as quoted in Itsiipootsikimskai 2023). The whole universe, from the sky beings to the earth beings and the occupant's power, is represented by a spirit animal who has given them access to their powers to help them in their lives (Glenbow 2013). There are transfer songs and ceremonies specifically associated with that design. There are protocols for setting them up and for being inside of them. It is considered disrespectful to step over the lodge poles: one should go around them. There are protocols for harvesting the materials to construct the tipi such as the poles and pegs. There are stories that go *way* back regarding which types of wood can be used, and the construction of the dwelling is a kind of ceremony itself. There are also ceremonies that involve blessing these relatives, talking to them, like in the case of the Ookan being constructed during Akoka'tssin (Many Lodges Camp or "Sundance") "We're gonna take you and use you for the center pole" (Ninna Piiksii/Bruised Head, oral teaching, December 28, 2020). Tipis and other Blackfoot structures illustrate how, for many Indigenous Peoples, a structure is not simply a structure but involves relationship and reciprocity.

Relational Math

Blackfoot scholar Dr. Leroy Little Bear (pers. comm., October 11, 2019) shared his perspectives about math and measurement, concluding that Western science relies on math to quantify the natural world and the cosmos. Consequently, because Indigenous people are not thought to be mathematical, Westerners (or Western-oriented people) think Indigenous people are not scientific. He said that from a Western perspective that may be true; however, "when you have a very different type of science that is not based on quantification but is based on relationships, do you need all that math?" He argues that "math arises out of a need" and out of lack or loss of relationship with natural and cosmic beings—all my relatives (Little Bear 2011, 2015, 2016). Number is only one kind of being with whom Indigenous people have relationships, and as such for Niitsitapi, math is only one part of their science rather than the foundation of all STEM knowledge and proofs as in the West. Ihtsipaitapiiyo'pa lives in every form of creation—including numbers, as all life forms contribute and participate in giving life and knowledge. Bastien and Mistaken Chief (2004) confirm Little Bear's views that knowing is relational, explaining that "knowing is dependent upon relationships, which create and *generate* knowledge" (77). This is fascinating and powerful; the idea of knowledge not just waiting to be discovered but rather knowledge being created and generated in an ongoing way as a result of participation and relationship with all the relatives—expanding like the universe itself. In his autobiography *The Meaning and Limits of Exact Science,* nineteenth-century physicist Max Planck (1949) makes a connection between relationship and measurement, stating, "An experiment is a question which science poses to Nature, and a measurement is the recording of Nature's answer" (110). Bastien and Mistaken Chief (2004) continue, describing the role of dreams and lived experience as a means for knowledge to be revealed, once again tying knowing with being and doing and the inseparability of knowing and observations, stories, and spiritual revelation:

> All our life experiences are a source of knowledge. As an example, dreams are a primary source of knowledge. . . . Often dreams are prophetic, contain warnings, or reveal knowledge. Such dreams are passed on through the oral traditions among the people and are repeatedly found in stories

and ceremonies. . . . Dreams like this provide guidance and protection. The individual is shown gifts that can be pursued. If they are accepted, then the individual will be protected. More importantly, dreams reveal knowledge that guides us in our personal responsibilities (Kiitomohpiipotokoi) in life. (Bastien and Mistaken Chief 2004, 77–79)

Hanohano (1999) submits that without acknowledging and engaging spirit, there can be no meaningful Indigenization of education, explaining that "calls for reforming our educational systems to better meet the needs of Native students always include Native culture and language. And the most distinguishing feature of Native culture and language is its spirituality. However, this is the one aspect of Native culture that is often missing, neglected, or dismissed in western educational models" (211).

Reflecting on Niitsitapi numeracy, Little Bear (2019) asks the question, "What is the deep meaning of 7? Is 7 a name for anything? In Native counting systems the numbers are actually names for things. They are named numerals." He explains that Blackfoot and other Native languages are verb-rich, "action is embedded in nouns." The action of counting fingers and toes gives them a base-ten system, the name/story for Six translates as "cross over to the other hand," while Nine's name/story is subtractive: "one before the end of the hands." Ni't (or "nitokska") means one (whole), 1, or only; niit is a root word for real; niitsii truth; and niitaapi means the way it is; it is real; or it is true. Four represents balance and wholeness but one *is* wholeness, truth, and reality, and this is reflected in the way all other numbers to infinity are always in relation to 1 or oneness. He differentiates modern math as a subject and tool from the essence of math saying, "The cosmos is mathematical, if we are talking about mathematics as beauty, simplicity, unity." Citing Closs (1986), Little Bear shares the story of the conflicting perspectives surrounding the James Bay hydroelectric project where an Elder was asked to tell how many rivers there were in the area, and he couldn't. The scientist thought he had made his point, but it turns out the Elder had a relationship with each river and knew them intimately by name and character; he therefore did not need to count them. Little Bear summarizes that "assembly lines demand counting, relationships don't," maintaining that Blackfoot reasons for using math are relational not mechanical. Little Bear submits that even the Greeks had the Golden Ratio,[5] which suggests their math began as Greeks noticing relationships in nature. Little Bear (2015) then postulates that "what is possible in Blackfoot may not be possible in English" implying that without the Blackfoot language, numbers lose their meaning/stories and become little more than symbols of specific quantities as math gets superimposed on nature rather than something inherent in nature.

Werner Heisenberg (1990), father of quantum mechanics, in correspondence with Albert Einstein, expressed how shocked, frightened, and unprepared he was to discover the wholeness and relationship that nature presented to them:

> If nature leads us to mathematical forms of great simplicity and beauty—by forms, I am referring to coherent systems of hypotheses, axioms, etc.—to forms that no one has previously encountered, we cannot help thinking that they are "true," that they reveal a genuine feature of nature. . . . You must have felt this too: the almost frightening simplicity and *wholeness of the relationships* which nature suddenly spreads out before us and for which none of us was in the least prepared. (Heisenberg 1990, 65; emphasis added)

In Atwood's classroom, she found that students were generally more engaged and successful with applied and conceptual math than with facts and formulas. Examples include instances when learners could experience numbers not only as abstract equations, measurements, and quantities but names that describe relationships in nature, and when there were practical real-life applications for doing math.

Discussion

"Any group that wishes to be regarded as the authority in a human society must not simply banish or discredit the views of their rivals, they must become the sole source of truth for that society and defend their status and the power to interpret against all comers by providing the 'best' explanation of the data" (Deloria 1997, 26). The UNESCO and ICSU World Conference on Science's (2000) claim that "modern science does not constitute the only form of knowledge" may seem innocuous enough, yet the greatest opposition to fundamentally decolonizing and Indigenizing or transforming STEM curriculum and pedagogy is the concern that acknowledging the spiritual processes and spiritual realities that are indispensable to IWKB will compromise the "purity" of Western science, which has been achieved by approaching nature as objectively as possible. Consequently, overcoming entrenched stigmas that IWKB are unreliable become an obstacle. Another obstacle can be gaining access to Indigenous Elders and knowledge keepers, or even vetted cultural resources needed to Indigenize STEM instruction meaningfully and respectfully. There is also the question of time constraints that limit adding new content to already distended curricular outcomes for each grade. Deloria (1977) asserts that the "fundamental factor that keeps Indians and non-Indians from communicating is that they are speaking about two entirely different perceptions of the world" (vii). Little Bear

(2000) refers to this ontological-epistemological impasse as "jagged worldviews colliding." The results of this study—the theoretical framework we developed and concrete examples from Atwood's lived experience in the classroom—suggest that these very different worldviews can align in complementary ways that establish closer links between these and other "forms, systems and approaches to knowledge, for the mutual enrichment and benefit" of all learners (UNESCO and ICSU World Conference on Science 2000).

With the relatively new mandates and directives such as those found in the United Nations Declaration on the Rights of Indigenous Peoples (UNDRIP) in 2007, Canada's Truth and Reconciliation Commission (TRC) Calls to Action (2015), and the subsequent Alberta Teacher Quality Standard 5 (Alberta Education 2012) enacted by Ministerial Order in response to those calls to action (and similar standards, processes or policies enacted by other jurisdictions worldwide), K−12 and postsecondary educators are looking for ways forward to transform Western education. This study presents a way. One Elder recently said to Atwood, "You suspended your Western thought to learn our ways. Now you know your way and our way. What you're doing now is creating a third way" (Ninna Piiksii/Bruised Head 2021). Without overgeneralizing, there are some key steps we will highlight. Too often educators try to supplement or append the curriculum with Indigenous worldview "content." This can lead to "jagged" results that Little Bear (2000) talks about and can also lead to pan-Indigenizing the specific knowledges, languages, territories, and practices of distinct Indigenous groups. To align Western and Indigenous worldviews in more complementary (combine so as to enhance or emphasize the qualities of each other) ways, our research suggests starting where most Indigenous people start: relationship and alignment with each other and all one's relatives in their respective environments.

Relationship is always the first step. Blackfoot scholar Tsuaki Marule (2012) confirms, "For education to be meaningful, students and educators must form substantial relationships with one another as well as with the knowledge being transferred" (132). Building a sense of community among students is key, but also indispensable is the need to encourage personal connection and reflection with the subject matter or knowledge herself. Next, it is necessary to search out the concepts embedded in the objectives of a subject area in the curriculum. Imagine these concepts as being universal rather than focusing only on the Western connotations and contexts associated with the specific concepts. Then, instructors should teach those concepts from the perspective of at least two worldviews: Western and whichever Indigenous territory (or other non-Western culture) one is teaching. Even if the Indigenous population no longer occupies that territory, one should find out whose land they are on. The Alberta grade-three curriculum includes multiple worldviews, so Atwood included them also. Likewise, when Atwood has students who have immigrated from other locations or international students, she includes their worldviews as well: this creates space for them to make meaning of the subject that is consistent with their own ways of knowing and to further expand understanding of other knowledge systems. Think of an overarching conceptual question that encompasses all the concepts in the curricular objectives or borrow our question. This helps to overcome the way curricular objectives are often linear or organized in silos. Adding the word "relational" to each subject (e.g., relational science) signals and reminds students to consider their relationship with the knowledge and the relatives who gift us their knowledge. And most importantly, whenever possible one should seek out local Elders who can come into the classroom or at least share with the educator about their culture-specific understanding of comprehensive relational animacy and the protocols for initiating and renewing relationships with all the relatives. Indigenous learning is land-based, language-based, and culture-based so relationships with Elders and community members are important. However, the framework we developed can still be effectively adopted by simply creating space for things in nature to be alive and interrelated, which is a relatively generalizable tenet of most IWKB. This is enough to get started. Atwood recently co-presented with Blackfoot knowledge keeper and environmental scientist Lowell Yellow Horn at a divisional professional development session where thirty high school science teachers attended. Many saw the value in simply explaining to their students that for Blackfoot and many other Indigenous Peoples, everything is alive and interrelated in nonhierarchical ways. They welcomed the idea of encouraging their students, while learning about physics, biology, or chemistry to imagine what it might be like to be a beam of light or a beaver or a water molecule and to try to predict those relatives' behavior and understand why they behave the way they do through the Indigenous practice of aligning oneself with nature. This is the method in its essence, although it will and should vary from context to context.

Conclusion

Establishing closer links between IWKB and Western science requires teaching Niitsitapi and other Indigenous stories beyond the humanities classroom; better engaging etiological, ontological, epistemological, axiological, and practical traditions of Niitsitapi and other Indigenous Peoples; and operationalizing pedagogical and methodological models that acknowledge, respect, and embody Indigenous ways of knowing and being. This study presents a theoretical framework for STEM educators who don't typically engage with IWKB to weave relational ways of knowing into STEM concepts in the course objectives. It demonstrates through concrete examples, actionable steps to begin engaging with Indigenous knowledge systems in science, technology, engineering, and math.

SANDRA BARTLETT ATWOOD is an instructor of Indigenous studies, School of Arts and Sciences, Lethbridge College, Lethbridge, Canada.

NIINNA PIIKSII (CHIEF BIRD) MIKE BRUISED HEAD is a Blackfoot Awaaáhsskata (Grandfather/Elder); Chairman, Kainai Board of Education, Blood Reserve, Canada; Instructor, Werkland School of Education, University of Calgary, Calgary, Canada; and Elder Advisor, University of Lethbridge, Lethbridge, Canada.

MARK W. BRUNSON is a professor emeritus of environment and society, Utah State University, Logan.

AAHSAOPI (STATE OF BEING) LAVERNE FIRST RIDER is a Blackfoot Awaaáhsskata (Grandmother/Elder); and Kainai Studies Coordinator, Kainai Board of Education, Blood Reserve, Canada.

TIM FRANDY (Sámi American) is assistant professor in the Department of Central, Eastern, and Northern European Studies, University of British Columbia, Vancouver, Canada.

JAMES MAFFIE is a professor emeritus of history, philosophy and American studies, University of Maryland, College Park.

AAKAOMO'TSSTAKI (MANY VICTORIES) MICHELLE PROVOST is Director of Learning (Literacy and Math), Kainai Board of Education, Blood Reserve, Canada.

MIINIIPOKAA (BERRY CHILD) PETER WEASEL MOCCASIN is a Blackfoot Awaaáhsskata (Grandfather/Elder), Blood Reserve, Canada; Kaahsinnoonik (Grandparent/Mentor) and honorary degree holder, Applied Science-Ecosystem Management, Lethbridge College, Lethbridge, Canada.

References

Alberta Education. 2018. "Teacher Quality Standards." https://www.alberta.ca/assets/documents/ed-teaching-quality-standard-english-print-ready.pdf.

Allan, Bruce, Any Perreault, John Chenoweth, Dianne Biin, Sharon Hobenshield, Todd Ormiston, Shirley Anne Hardman, Louise Lacerte, Lucas Wright, and Justin Wilson. 2018. *Pulling Together: A Guide for Teachers and Instructors.* Victoria, BC: BCcampus Publishers. https://opentextbc.ca/indigenization instructors/.

Armitage, Derek, Fikret Berkes, Aaron Dale, Erik Kocho-Schellenberg, and Eva Patton. 2011. "Co-management and the Co-production of Knowledge: Learning to Adapt in Canada's Arctic." *Global Environmental Change* 21, no. 3: 995–1004.

Bastien, Betty, and Duane Mistaken Chief. 2004. *Blackfoot Ways of Knowing: The Worldview of the Siksikaitsitapi.* Calgary: University of Calgary Press.

Battiste, Marie, Lynne Bell, and L. M. Findlay. 2002. "Decolonizing Education in Canadian Universities: An Interdisciplinary, International, Indigenous Research Project." *Canadian Journal of Native Education* 26, no. 2: 82–95.

Battiste, Marie. 2013. *Decolonizing Education: Nourishing the Learning Spirit.* Vancouver: Purich Publishing.

Brinkmann, Malte, and Norm Friesen. 2018. "Phenomenology and Education." In *International Handbook of Philosophy of Education,* edited by P. Smeyers and P. Springer, 591–608. International Handbooks of Education. Cham: Springer.

Boremanse, Didier. 2000. "Sewing Machines and Q'echi' Maya Worldview." *Anthropology Today* 16, no. 1: 11–18.

Boroditsky, Lera. 2017. "How Language Shapes the Way We Think." *YouTube.* November 2017. https://www.ted.com/talks/lera_boroditsky_how_language _shapes_the_way_we_think.

Burkhart, Brian. 2019a. "Countering Epistemic Guardianship with Epistemic Sovereignty Through the Land." *Native American and Indigenous Philosophy* 18, no. 2: 2–7.

———. 2019b. *Indigenizing Philosophy Through the Land: A Trickster Methodology for Decolonizing Environmental Ethics and Indigenous Futures.* East Lansing: Michigan State University Press.

Cajete, Gregory. 1994. *Look to the Mountain: An Ecology of Indigenous Education.* Durango, CO: Kivaki Press.

———. 2000. *Native Science: Natural Laws of Interdependence.* Santa Fe, NM: Clear Light Books.

Chambers, David Wade, and Richard Gillespie. 2000. "Locality in the History of Science: Colonial Science, Technoscience, and Indigenous Knowledge. *Osiris* 15, no. 1: 221–40.

Closs, Michael P. 1986. *Native American Mathematics.* Austin: University of Texas Press.

Conference Board of Canada. n.d. "How Can More Indigenous People Access STEM Careers?" Accessed February 6, 2024. https://www.conferenceboard .ca/research/ how-can-more-indigenous-people-access-stem-careers.

Dear, Peter. 2006. *The Intelligibility of Nature: How Science Makes Sense of the World.* Chicago: University of Chicago Press.

Deloria, Vine Jr. 1977. *The Metaphysics of Modern Existence.* San Francisco: Harper and Row.

———. 1997. *Red Earth, White Lies: Native Americans and the Myth of Scientific Fact.* Golden, CO: Fulcrum.

———. 2004. "Marginal and Submarginal." In *Indigenizing the Academy: Transforming Scholarship and Empowering Communities,* edited by Mihesuah Devon Abbott and Angela Cavender Wilson, 16–30. Lincoln: University of Nebraska Press.

Dotson, Kristie. 2011. "Tracking Epistemic Violence: Tracking Practices of Silencing." *Hypatia a Journal of Feminist Philosophy* 26, no. 2: 236–57.

Eyring, Henry J. 2008. *Mormon Scientist: The Life and Faith of Henry Eyring.* Salt Lake City, UT: Deseret.

Fricker, Miranda. 2007. *Epistemic Injustice: Power and the Ethics of Knowing.* London: Oxford Press.

Gaudry, Adam, and Danielle Lorenz. 2018. "Indigenization as Inclusion, Reconciliation, and Decolonization: Navigating the Different Visions for Indigenizing the Canadian Academy." *AlterNative: An International Journal of Indigenous Peoples* 14, no. 3: 218–27.

Glenbow Museum Blackfoot Gallery Committee. 2013. *The Story of the Blackfoot People: Niitsitapiisinni.* Buffalo, NY: Firefly Books.

Hanohano, Peter. 1999. "The Spiritual Imperative of Native Epistemology: Restoring Harmony and Balance to Education." *Canadian Journal of Native Education* 23, no. 2: 206–19.

Hendon, Julia A. 2018. "Can Tools Have Souls? Maya Views of the Relations between Humans and Other-than-Human Persons." In *Other Than Human Agency,* edited by Eleanor Harrison-Buck and Julia A. Hendon, 147–66. Denver: University of Colorado Press.

Heisenberg, Werner. 1990. As quoted in *Truth and Beauty: Aesthetics and Motivations in Science* by S. Chandrasekhar. Chicago: University of Chicago Press.

Itsiipootsikimskai. 2023. "Níksókowaawák as Axiom: The Indispensability of Comprehensive Relational Animacy in Blackfoot Ways of Knowing, Being, and Doing." Society and Natural Resources. London: Taylor & Francis Online. https://www.tandfonline.com/doi/full/10.1080/08941920.2023.2180696.

Kimmerer, R. W. 2013. *Braiding Sweetgrass: Indigenous Wisdom, Scientific Knowledge, and the Teachings of Plants.* Minneapolis: Milkweed Editions.

LaDuke, Wintona. 1996. "Ecology and Spirituality: Following the Path of Natural Law." In *A Seat at the Table: Huston Smith in Conversation with Native Americans on Religious Freedom,* edited by Huston Smith 39–57. *Academia.* https://www.academia.edu/69186687/The_Religions_of_the_Native _Americans_REL_3573_29212_Course_Syllabus_.

Latulippe, Nicole, and Nicole Klenk. 2020. "Making Room and Moving Over: Knowledge Co-production, Indigenous Knowledge Sovereignty and the Politics of Global Environmental Change Decision-Making." *Current Opinion in Environmental Sustainability* 42: 7–14.

Lindstrom, Gabrielle, Cash Ahenakew, Betty Bastien, Audrey Weasel Traveller, Michelle Provost, Lynden (Lyndsay) Crowshoe, and J. Smith. 2021. *Misaamokaksin: Transitioning and Transforming Treaty-Based Education.* Brocket, AB: Peigan Board of Education.

Little Bear, Leroy. 2000. "Jagged Worldviews Collide." In *Reclaiming Indigenous Voice and Vision,* edited by Marie Battiste, 77–85. Vancouver: University of British Columbia Press.

———. 2011. "Native and Western Science: Possibilities in a Dynamic Collaboration. YouTube. May 9. https://www.youtube.com/watch?v=ycQtQZ9y3lc&ab_channel=ArizonaStateUniversity.

———. 2015. "Indigenous Knowledge and Western Science." YouTube, January 14. https://www.youtube.com/watch?v=gJSJ28eEUjI.

———. 2016. "Big Thinking: Blackfoot Metaphysics 'Waiting in the Wings'." YouTube. June 1. https://www.youtube.com/watch?v=o_txPA8CiA4.

Maurial, Mahia. 1999. "Indigenous Knowledge and Schooling: A Continuum Between Conflict and Dialogue." In *What is Indigenous Knowledge: Voices from the Academy,* edited by Ladislaus M. Semali and Joe L. Kincheloe, 59–77. New York: Falmer Press.

May, Howard. 2022. "Southern Alberta Man Recruits Beavers to Build Him a Dam." *Town & Country Today.* November 10. https://www.albertaprimetimes.com/beyond-local/southern-alberta-man-recruits-beavers-to-build-him-a-dam-6084768.

Marule, Tsuaki R. O. 2012. "Niitsitapi Relational and Experiential Theories in Education." *Open Journal Systems UBC* 35, no. 1: 131–43. https://www.Downloads/cncon,+10.+Niitsitapi+Relational+and+Experiential+Theories+in+Education.pdf.

Meadow, Alison M., Daniel B. Ferguson, Zack Guido, Alexandra Horangic, Gigi Owen, and Tamara Wall. 2015. "Moving toward the Deliberate Coproduction of Climate Science Knowledge." *Weather, Climate, and Society* 7, no. 2: 170–91.

Nadasdy, Paul. 1999. "The Politics of TEK: Power and the "Integration" of Knowledge." *Arctic Anthropology* 36 (1/2): 1–18.

National Museums Scotland. 2022. "Concepts Have Teeth: Blackfoot Objects at National Museums." January 24. https://blog.nms.ac.uk/2022/01/24/concepts-have-teeth-blackfoot-objects-at-national-museums-scotland/#:~:text=It%20is%20hard%20to%20express,children%20who%20were%20taken%20away.

Planck, Max. 1949. "The Meaning and Limits of Exact Science." *Science* 110, no. 2857 (September 30): 325.

Picard, Martin, and Carmen Sandi. 2021. "The Social Nature of Mitochondria: Implications for Human Health." *Neuroscience Biobehavioral Review* 1, no. 120: 595–610.

Reed, Ron, and Kari Norgaard. 2021. "Fire Is Food: A Virtual Brown Bag Discussion with Ron Reed and Kari Norgaard." *Ethnic Studies Review* 44, no. 2: 5–18.

Rittel, Horst W. J., and Melvin M. Webber. 1973. "Dilemmas in a General Theory of Planning." *Policy Sciences* 4, no. 2: 155–69.

Smith, Linda Tuhiwai. 2012. *Decolonizing Methodologies: Research and Indigenous Peoples.* London: Zed Books.

Spivak, Gayatri Chakravorty. 1988. "Can the Subaltern Speak?" In *Marxism and the Interpretation of Culture,* edited by Cary Nelson and Lawrence Grossberg, 271–313. Urbana: University of Illinois Press.

Stantec Native Program. 2021. "Stantec Native Program Strives to Effect Change within the Native Population and Create a Path to STEM Careers." Stantec. September 21. https://www.stantec.com/en/ideas/content/careers/2021/indigenizing-the-future-of-stem-stantecs-alaska-native-program.

Stewart, Georgina. 2007. *"Kaupapa Māori Science."* PhD diss., University of Waikato, Hamilton, New Zealand. https://hdl.handle.net/10289/2598.

———. 2023. "Why There Are So Few Māori in Science." *NZ News.* May 22. https://www.stuff.co.nz/opinion/300883336/why-there-are-so-few-mori-in-science.

Strevens, Michael. 2020. *The Knowledge Machine: How Irrationality Created Modern Science.* New York: Liveright Publishing.

Truth and Reconciliation Commission of Canada: Calls to Action. 2015. https://ehprnh2mwo3.exactdn.com/wpcontent/uploads/2021/01/Calls_to_Action_English2.pdf.

UNESCO and ICSU. 2002. "World Conference on Science for the Twenty-First Century: A New Commitment." https://unesdoc.unesco.org/ark:/48223/pf0000120706.

United Nations. 2007. "Declaration on the Rights of Indigenous People." New York: United Nations. https://www.un.org/development/desa/indigenouspeoples/wpcontent/uploads/sites/19/2018/11/UNDRIP_E_web.pdf.

Wilson, Shawn. 2008. *Research is Ceremony: Indigenous Research Methods.* Winnipeg: Fernwood Publishing.

Notes

We gratefully acknowledge the Blackfoot community for their patience and generosity in sharing some of their stories with the non-Native authors in the collective and for the way those stories have guided and informed this research.

1. Four of the authors are Blackfoot. One author, Tim Frandy, is Sámi American, and the remaining three authors are of various mixed settler descent. All authors contributed collectively and are listed alphabetically. The group formed an alliance and took the name Itsiipootsikimskai (Where Waters Come Together as Friends, or Confluence). Itsiipootsikimskai is the collective name by which this essay should be cited, i.e., Itsiipootsikimskai 2024 as opposed to Atwood et al. 2024.

2. With permission from Blackfoot Elder, Aiaistahkommi (Shoots at Close Range)/Duane Mistaken Chief (Facebook message, February 17, 2024) and following the late Betty Bastien's intention that she voiced to Duane that "it was always our book," we have cited Duane as a co-author. There is also a precedent for this in https://www.mtroyal.ca/nonprofit/InstituteforCommunityProsperity/_pdfs/Tim-Curren_Learning-and-Connecting-With-the-Land_Scholarly-Output.pdf.

3. As given to Atwood by Blood Tribe Chief, Makiinima (Curlew) Roy Fox, January 27, 2023, while Fox was sharing the story of his name.

4. As defined in Bastien and Mistaken Chief (2004, 211).

5. The golden ratio, also referred to as the divine proportion, is a special attribute denoted by the Greek symbol φ. It is approximately equal to 1.618 and appears often in nature, mathematics, geometry, art, architecture. For instance, the Parthenon and the Great Pyramid of Egypt.

ROBERT LEE

Seeing Red: Indigenous Land, American Expansion, and the
   Political Economy of Plunder in North America
by Michael John Witgen
University of North Carolina Press, 2022

SEEING RED IS an impressive book. In this work, Witgen examines the colonization of Anishinaabeg territory by the United States from the 1780s to the 1850s. His analysis homes in on mixed-race individuals, paying close attention to law and belonging. The book is especially notable for its innovative conceptualization of the engine that facilitated U.S. expansion and positioned Native communities to resist removal.

Witgen calls that engine the "political economy of plunder," an evocative name applied to the operation of the treaty system in the western Great Lakes. Scholars are accustomed to approaching the Treaty of Saginaw (1819) or the Treaty of Washington (1836) as coercive. Witgen argues these and others also functioned as subsidies for an encroaching settler society. Because the fur trade that predominated in the northern reaches of the "Old Northwest" required Indigenous labor and coopted annuity payments to service debts, U.S. colonialism mixed extractive features with a drive to eliminate. Witgen contrasts this situation to southeastern North America, where the United States functioned more like a quintessential settler colonial state determined to redistribute Native land quickly and convert its use to cotton cultivation.

Across five substantial chapters, Witgen examines the plunder economy's rise and navigation by tribal nations. He starts with the legal and cultural logic of the U.S. settler state, revisiting federal policy inflection points, from the Northwest Ordinance to Indian Removal, to argue that the United States was born as a colonial power seeking to subordinate Indigenous resources. Next, he employs the life story of Zhaazhaawanibiisens (aka John Tanner) to enter the "Native New World" and explain how the treaty system grafted onto the fur trade. He then zeroes in on settler intermarriages with

Native women, unions that served as conduits of influence. Although mixed-race individuals were critical to the function of the region's economy as kin, interpreters, and traders, they were problematic for U.S. jurisprudence, a tension investigated in the final two chapters through the murder trial of Chigawaaskiing and the contested treaty rights of "half-breeds." A conclusion examines the creation of the Lake Superior Chippewa reservation at La Pointe as a successful instance of resistance to removal, tempered by legislative support that prioritized ongoing access to annuity wealth for settlers. If there is a shortcoming here, it is one of omission toward the end. Neither the fur trade nor annuities lasted, but the consequences of their disappearance receive scant attention.

A brief review cannot do justice to the complex narrative presented in *Seeing Red.* One critical element that merits widespread attention—and that links it to recent scholarship by Anne Hyde, Lucy Eldersveld Murphy, and Bethel Saler—is Witgen's emphasis on mixed-race families. Witgen stresses the key roles individuals with ties linking Anishinaabeg communities, fur trade outfits, and settler governments played in U.S. colonization as negotiators and claimants of treaty rights. He likewise attends to the pressures they faced when choosing between racialized colonial subjecthood and social acceptance in white settler society. Witgen observes that for mixed-race Anishinaabeg people, obtaining standing in the United States often demanded the denial of Native identities and the dispossession of kin but also helped to ensure regional survivance. The point is neither to vilify nor excuse the choices made but to call out the "authenticity trap" as a mechanism in a system of white wealth creation that operated not just by taking Native property, but by drawing on the presence of Native people pigeonholed as a race lacking property rights.

The sheer resonance of Witgen's conceptual apparatus is also a highly noteworthy feature of *Seeing Red.* In that sense, the "political economy of plunder" is reminiscent of another idea from Great Lakes historiography: Richard White's influential concept of the "middle ground," which inspired scholars to locate cognate sites of encounter across time and space, loosening the term's analytical precision in the process. One wonders if the "plunder economy" will face a similar pull between specific and general applicability as it shapes the historical imagination. Conceived as the expropriation of Indigenous wealth, plunder went hand in glove with U.S. expansion and racialization, and it continues today. Witgen pushes the concept into a national frame. Others may take it further. One could argue that colonial regimes around the world and across centuries built political economies of plunder based on Indigenous resource theft. The trade-off to doing so will be to broaden the definition of the "plunder economy" in ways that dilute its explanatory power for understanding the interaction between the treaty system and the fur trade that structured the transformation of Anishinaabeg territory.

Wherever that discussion goes, it will speak to the magnitude of Witgen's accomplishment. *Seeing Red* deserves careful reading by scholars concerned with Anishinaabe history, U.S. expansion, and colonial resource extraction in North America and beyond.

ROBERT LEE is associate professor of history at the University of Cambridge.

REBECCA HALL

Upholding Indigenous Economic Relationships: Nehiyawak Narratives
by Shalene Wuttunee Jobin
University of British Columbia Press, 2023

FROM THE OPENING PARAGRAPHS of *Upholding Indigenous Economic Relationships: Nehiyawak Narratives*, Shalene Wuttunee Jobin's words find strength and clarity in their groundedness. Jobin is a member of the Red Pheasant Cree Nation, and her analysis grows out of her kin and community relations, an expansion of the economic through an attention to Nehiyawak (Cree) relations and principles. From this grounding, these words offer insight that reverberates across disciplines and readership, contributing a novel analysis of the tight threads that bind colonialism and capitalism, as well as modes of living and reproducing Indigenous economic relationships in the context of and in resistance to settler-colonial Canada.

In *Upholding Indigenous Economic Relationships*, Jobin takes on two intersecting projects. The first is an intervention into analysis of the economic exploitation of Indigenous Peoples in Canada. She argues that while colonialism is often understood in largely sociopolitical terms, "economic exploitation was the first and most enduring relationship between newcomers and Indigenous Peoples" (25). The enduring quality of colonial economic exploitation and its inextricability from settler state formations shape Jobin's assessment of contemporary Indigenous/settler relations in Canada. Like many of the scholars in the critical Indigenous political economy literature (e.g., Glen Coulthard, Rauna Kuokkanen, and Isabel Altamirano-Jiménez), Jobin is skeptical of contemporary approaches to Indigenous self-determination that position the capitalist market as a mode of escape from a paternalistic settler state. Rather, Jobin argues that centuries of capitalist exploitation have constricted the possibilities of economic independence to an economy in capital's image *only*. She writes, "Simply stated, the answer is not trading state colonialism for capitalist colonialism" (25).

For Jobin, the contemporary focus on Indigenous economic independence is limited by a foreclosure of possibilities for the sake of reproducing settler capitalist political economies, here in their neoliberal iteration. Challenging this limited vision, the second project that Jobin undertakes in this text is to make visible Indigenous economic systems, past and present, and to reflect on resurgent practices grounded in Nehiyawak economic principles and oriented toward reproducing Nehiyawak relationships. Jobin asserts and honors autonomous Indigenous economic relationships through both historical narrative and grounded theory. This intimacy between past and present (and, arguably, future) shapes Jobin's theory of Cree economic relations as well. Crucially, writing against the deflating settler conflation of land with property, Jobin theorizes Cree relations to land as both economic—from the personal to the life-sustaining—and more than economic. In analyzing contemporary enactments of Nehiyawak economic principles as resurgent practices, Jobin honors community labors, like the Giveaway Ceremony and cooperative gardening.

Jobin's approach to resurgence is both generous and nuanced. She allows herself and her reader to get messy, to write from within "contaminated times" (Lyons 2010). Jobin writes from Treaty 6 Territory, a region that has borne an intensified expression of settler Canada's extractive economy: here, in the form of oil and gas. These contaminants infiltrate her writing as they infiltrate the lives of the human and nonhuman animals of the land. She takes up resurgent practices, not as ideals existing beyond extractive biophysical and existential contaminants but as real practices that emerge from within and alongside them. Engaging with literature of cognitive dissonance, she writes about the *colonial* dissonance that comes from centuries of colonial violence, including, in its neoliberal forms, the incorporation of Indigenous workers into extractive regimes that alter "their relationship to the land" (142). Writing against a fatalistic approach to the contradictions of colonial capitalism, Jobin asks her reader to turn to the creative possibilities in moving through colonialism's dissonances, using Nehiyawak principles as a guide.

In all her writing, Jobin does the double work of marking out resurgent pathways while walking them herself. Just as her theory is grounded in her relations to community, so, too, is her writing, and the book is graced with windows into her writing spaces, both ecological and interior. Likewise, the book's commitment to Nehiyawak knowledge is written in its syllabics, sharing linguistic knowledge that deeply enriches the text. Ultimately, Jobin writes that while this book centers Nehiyawak relationships, she hopes it will be useful to other communities. I have no doubt this will be the case. Jobin's combination of accessible and lively writing with deep, careful analysis will make this book of interest to both academics and activists alike, to those who see their own community reflected in this work, and those seeking to learn about the rich economic relationships of the Cree People. This is an essential and generous text, offering a rich contribution to analyses of capitalist colonialism and resurgent pathways of life-making that exist within and beyond our colonial present.

REBECCA HALL is associate professor in the Department of Global Development Studies at Queen's University in Ontario, Canada.

ROBBIE ETHRIDGE

Talking Back: Native Women and the Making of the Early South
by Alejandra Dubcovsky
Yale University Press, 2023

IN *TALKING BACK: Native Women and the Making of the Early South,* historian
Alejandra Dubcovsky builds on her prodigious knowledge and understanding of the early colonial South, Spanish Florida, and the multiethnic social
matrix of the times and place to re-cover the lives and histories of women
living there. In so doing, she definitively demonstrates that despite the usual
silences and ellipses of women in archival sources, women were central to
both large and small events in the early South. *Talking Back* follows women's
lives from 1690 to the 1710s—these were the years, as Dubcovsky explains,
leading up to, during, and immediately after Queen Anne's War (the War of
Spanish Succession). This war, Dubcovsky points out, was not solely a European conflict, and in the American South it spun into a frenzy of opportu-
nistic enslavements, Indigenous intergroup conflicts, and a contest between
the English and Spanish. Her goal, though, is not to rewrite the history of
Queen Anne's War, but rather to place women at the center of the conflict,
to delineate their options, and to understand how and when they exercised
those options.

Dubcovsky is a dynamite writer; I consider her one of the finest in the
business of American history. Her intelligent organization, quick pacing,
smart phrasing, and expansive vocabulary make for captivating and lively
writing and absorbing reading for both specialists and non-specialists.

Dubcovsky's fine-mesh sifting of archival sources for mentions of women,
no matter how slight, demonstrates that it is always worth the effort to
find them. And she finds many women, more than one might expect for this
early period. Snippets of the lives of the Yndia Chacata, María Magdalena,
María Jacoba, Chicuta Francisca, Ychu Francisca, Afac Gabriela, and Doña
Juana, among others, move into our historical line of sight and consciousness. Dubcovsky does not relay simple biographies of these women. Rather,
she tells their stories in a way that also unfolds the connectivity between
Native, Spanish, and African communities, the centrality of women to these
communities, and the large and small historical forces sweeping through
them during a particularly tumultuous time. Through the telling, Dubcovsky
imparts a deep understanding of the context and social history of early

colonial Spanish Florida and the conflict that consumed the region in the late seventeenth and early eighteenth centuries. She undergirds all of this with feminist theory, gender studies methodologies, and deft linguistic analysis to render a sophisticated and complex narrative about how gender dynamics and women's lives were both shaped by and shaped the history of the early colonial South.

The subtitle of the book "Native Women and the Making of the Early South," is a bit of a misnomer, though, since *Talking Back* includes women across the social and political spectrum who were living in Spanish Florida—Native women, African women, enslaved women, free women, elite Criollo women, and common European women. Dubcovsky reconstructs the multi-ethnic female population of Spanish Florida, their myriad and varied hopes and dreams, their common woes and difficulties, and their utter willfulness in a male-dominated, violent, and colonial regime. In fact, Dubcovsky's singular insight and originality is that she places all these women in conversation with one another. She paints intimate portraits of women in all stations of life and in all phases of their own lives, demonstrating how the conflicts in Queen Anne's War affected women differently depending on these factors and how their lives, regardless of the differences, intersected and were interconnected. It is a remarkable, sympathetic, and well-evidenced historical reconstruction of gender dynamics and the sometimes expected and sometimes surprising place of women in a colonial context.

ROBBIE ETHRIDGE is Professor Emerita of anthropology at the University of Mississippi.

LISA BLEE

Memory Wars: Settlers and Natives Remember Washington's
  Sullivan Expedition of 1779
by A. Lynn Smith
University of Nebraska Press, 2023

IN 1779, George Washington commanded General John Sullivan to attack Six Nations dwellings, crops, and orchards with the stated objective of causing "total destruction and devastation" (4). Sullivan's troops displaced hundreds of Indigenous people whose suffering was then compounded by disease, starvation, and exposure. In *Memory Wars,* A. Lynn Smith seeks to both historicize Euro-Americans' efforts to honor the Sullivan Expedition with monuments, markers, place names, and reenactments, and to understand how contemporary residents of the region embrace, challenge, or otherwise wrestle with the stories these memorials tell.

The book contains thirteen chapters organized into three parts: "Origins," "Reverberations," and "Interventions." The first and most substantial part, which is based on impressive historical research, details the construction of settler historical consciousness around the Sullivan campaign through the 1920s. Although these memorializing efforts were uncoordinated and emerged independently throughout the region, Smith contends that the "Sullivan commemorative complex" represents a cohesive celebration of settler-style colonialism. As such, its individual elements consistently reproduced narratives of Native elimination and settler-colonist replacement. Smith consciously builds upon Jean O'Brien's (2010) *Firsting and Lasting* by showing that the settler impulse to narrate Native people out of existence extended beyond New England but nevertheless emerged from localized white settler commitments.

Smith underscores regional difference by dividing the book into separate case studies of historical consciousness in Pennsylvania and New York, respectively. While Pennsylvanians told the story of the Sullivan Expedition through the lens of retribution for the "Wyoming Massacre" (an event better understood in the context of a conflict between colonist groups), New Yorkers considered the "Sullivan-Clinton Campaign" a victorious battle in a race war that cleared the region for white settlers. That is not to say these stories drew consensus; in New York, memorialists wrestled with the justice of a scorched-earth campaign targeting civilians. But their sympathy had its limits. Was it just a coincidence, Smith suggestively asks, that the Six Nations' 1919–1929 land claim movement coincided exactly with the New York state historian's planned programming commemorating the 150th anniversary of the Sullivan Expedition?

Following this fascinating historical reconstruction of settler historical consciousness, Smith devotes the second part of the book to contemporary engagements with Sullivan campaign stories. Smith interviews residents about battle reenactments, commemorative practices, and monuments. She finds that non-Natives in New York and Pennsylvania continue to deploy distinct historical frameworks to understand the expedition, while Native respondents in both states challenge the story in largely consistent terms. Smith especially highlights the work of non-Native organizations and individuals devoted to educating white neighbors and changing the dominant narrative.

Smith utilizes the ethnographic method to explore long-term reverberations of the Sullivan commemorative complex while wrestling with the ethical implications of asking Six Nations citizens for their thoughts on this painful story (which readers may expect, given the book's subtitle). She explains that as a non-Native anthropologist, she has chosen to only focus upon the "*public* manifestations of the Sullivan story" (301). Of course, settler-colonial stories and perspectives have long dominated the public realm, as the lengthy first part of the book demonstrates. Some readers may applaud her focus on settler memory. Others may see it as a missed opportunity to question the perception of domination and ask whether collaboration with Native scholars may have allowed for deeper engagement with contemporary perspectives. I should note that in acknowledging this latter critique, Smith directs readers to the work of Haudenosaunee historian Alyssa Mt. Pleasant.

That said, the book's third and final part engages with current Haudenosaunee public intellectuals and offers excellent insight into the operations of settler time and memory. Smith focuses on four Iroquoian cultural centers and interviews Haudenosaunee historians who have contributed to the exhibits and programming. She finds that the professionals at these centers deeply contextualize the Sullivan Expedition—when they mention it at all. Their approach disrupts the settler narrative of decline and replacement by "proclaiming [. . .] Haudenosaunee survivance" (328). At the Seneca Art & Culture Center at Ganondagan, for example, site manager G. Peter Jemison pointed out that the exhibits focus on the land sales that occurred *after* the Revolutionary War because those events played a central role in removing Seneca from their lands and limiting their ongoing efforts to protect their homes. "By not telling the Sullivan story," Smith concludes, "Ganondagan is able to tell so much more" (324).

Memory Wars is a well-written and uniquely organized interdisciplinary monograph that productively engages recent colonial studies and memory studies. Smith's work contributes to our understanding of regionally distinctive forms of settler historical consciousness emerging from difficult histories of violence and forced removal.

LISA BLEE is professor of history at Wake Forest University.

LINDSAY BORROWS

Reclaiming Anishinaabe Law: Kinamaadiwin Inaakonigewin and the Treaty Right to Education
by Leo Baskatawang
University of Manitoba Press, 2023

THROUGH A CAREFUL EXAMINATION of the neglected treaty relationship between the Crown and the Anishinaabe of Treaty 3, *Reclaiming Anishinaabe Law: Kinamaadiwin Inaakonigewin and the Treaty Right to Education* skilfully synthesizes a vision of Anishinaabe law as expressed through the current act of cultural resurgence known as the *Kinamaadiwin Inaakonigewin*—the Treaty 3 Anishinaabe Education Law. Dr. Leo Baskatawang opens his book with an analysis of colonialism's devastating attack on Indigenous education through tools of dispossession such as the *Indian Act,* residential schools, and overarching policy frameworks that inhibit Anishinaabe ways of knowing, being, doing, relating, and connecting to our lands. He points out that without a focus on revitalizing Indigenous Peoples' own education laws, future losses will include Indigenous languages, legal orders, and land-based knowledges—all of which are greatly needed in solving challenges both locally and globally.

Chapter 1 draws on the Anishinaabe understanding of the windigo—a being who has become dangerous and cannibalistic—to analogize how systems of colonization have impacted Indigenous lifeways particularly in the realm of education. The *Kinamaadiwin Inaakonigewin* is one important act of resurgence of Treaty 3 Anishinaabe traditional practices and epistemologies. It creates a legal framework to uphold Anishinaabe ways of learning and teaching to reclaim culturally relevant education and heal wounds inflicted by the windigo-like Canadian legal order that has instituted the miseducation of Indigenous Peoples for centuries.

Chapter 2 presents the historical legal context that frames the discussion on creating a contemporary Anishinaabe education law today. Dr. Baskatawang outlines four orders of Anishinaabe law. First, Kagagiwe Inaakonigewin, or Sacred Laws, which are forbidden to be written due to their sanctity. The second order he identifies is Kete Inaakonigewin (traditional laws), which are dedicated to the maintenance of cultural protocols and that he says are also not permitted to be written. The third order of Anishinaabe law he describes is Anishinaabe Inaakonigewin, or customary law. These laws are held by community members who practice long-standing ways of being and knowing in relation with the land. The fourth order of Anishinaabe law is Ozhibiige Inaakonigewin, which is written temporal law. The *Kinamaadiwin Inaakonigewin* is informed by all these orders, but it is expressed through the fourth order aimed at harmonization with the administration of other laws, such as Crown law.

There are important discussions in nearly every chapter of this book about what it means to write down or codify Anishinaabe law, given that historically it was nontextual. Dr. Baskatawang makes a persuasive case that it is a necessary element of legal revitalization today, despite the imperfections of writing down Anishinaabe laws (especially in English). He critiques an originalist vision that may freeze Indigenous legal traditions in time, unable to grow and adapt to changing circumstances. His views tend toward nuance and are alive to the interrelational nature of law and governance, particularly through Crown-Indigenous Treaty making, which he explores in depth in chapter 3.

This chapter invites the reader into an understanding of the history of treaties in Canada more broadly and then focuses in on Treaty 3. The author lays out an argument for why a treaty right to education exists. Chapter 4 then discusses why reconciliation must include recognition and affirmation of Indigenous laws by the Canadian state, including the *Kinamaadiwin Inaakonigewin.* There are various tools Indigenous Peoples use to advocate for change (including turning away from the state, negotiation, direct action etc.), and he frames this education law as one of many strategies needed to further self-determination. Dr. Baskatawang finds space for both a grassroots approach to revitalizing Anishinaabe law, while strongly advocating for state recognition and affirmation.

This book will be valuable as an introductory text for students learning about Indigenous Peoples and the Canadian legal system. Its strength is in thoroughly engaging with existing scholarly literature to summarize the field. I look forward to the author's further analysis and theorizing on the internal challenges of revitalizing Anishinaabe law. The reader is left wondering how communities within Treaty 3 worked out their differences of opinion in these vital matters. Dr. Baskatawang concludes his book with an offering of gratitude for the immense privilege to participate in the resurgence work of Anishinaabe education laws aimed at creating a better world for future generations. Readers, too, are left with a feeling of gratitude for the careful thought that went into this research, and for the essential work happening in Treaty 3 as they reclaim Anishinaabe ways of teaching, learning, and governing.

LINDSAY BORROWS is assistant professor of law at Queen's University, Ontario, Canada.

DANIEL RADUS

Indigenuity: Native Craftwork & the Art of American Literatures
by Caroline Wigginton
University of North Carolina Press, 2022

IN *INDIGENUITY*, Caroline Wigginton argues that in the settler-colonial literatures of North America there endures a "foundational but often hidden" relation to Native "craftwork," a term she uses to define utilitarian and decorative objects made by Indigenous Peoples (1). Wigginton refers to this relation throughout as an "orientation," a notable if unexplained choice that seems integral to her claims. In noting that literature orients itself to Indigenous craftwork, Wigginton refuses cognate terms—*engage* or *inform*, for instance—that would fail to reflect the intellectual ambition of her project. *Indigenuity* is not about references to Indigenous craftwork in settler-colonial literatures, though Wigginton describes these with precision and in abundance. Rather, Wigginton uses these references to offer a more sophisticated claim. In "the practices and objects of Native craftwork," she argues, is an archive of "aesthetic and sensory knowledge" that shaped "Europeans' efforts to construct their own relationships to Indigenous place" (13). These "sensations and emotions" are constitutive of settler literatures and, moreover, of "how settler colonists experienced and located themselves as bodies in Native lands" (15). Thus *Indigenuity* argues credibly that it is impossible to understand settler literatures—and, indeed, their important role in the settler-colonial project—without attention to the production, use, and ubiquitous presence of Indigenous material objects.

In establishing this constitutive relation, *Indigenuity* contributes to what seems the central thrust of several recent and important books, all of which use the methods of Indigenous studies to offer intricate analyses of the early (i.e., pre-1900) literatures of the present-day United States. Much like Angela Calcaterra's *Literary Indians* (2019) and Kelly Wisecup's *Assembled for Use* (2021), *Indigenuity* insists that settler literatures exist in constant and often confused negotiation with Native peoples and their expressive customs. And like these studies, too, *Indigenuity* argues that these negotiations were never unidirectional. Essential to *Indigenuity* is a parallel "narrative of Indigenous aesthetic repatriation" in which Native peoples exploited "the colonialist archive, restoring and supplementing ancestral knowledge and their own founts of innovation" (2). Thus while the first three chapters of the book focus on settler-produced texts, the last two reverse this course, focusing instead on those produced by Native peoples. The fourth, for example, concerns what Wigginton calls "hymncraft," the creation of music books that, in their veneration of "sacred relationships," fostered "new visions" of communal life for the Native Christians of Brothertown (17). And the fifth considers the book illustrations of Angel de Cora, the Ho-Chunk artist who, as Wigginton argues, affirms in her creative practice that Native craftwork was coextensive with the creation of books, not antecedent to it, and thus that Native artistic customs could endure beside "the benefits of the modern age" (160). These chapters exist in productive tension with the earlier three; taken as a whole, the structure of *Indigenuity* establishes that, as Wigginton observes, both settlers and Native peoples "bound craftwork and literature," though often to disparate ends (2).

But perhaps this description of *Indigenuity*'s structure is too facile. Though in the initial chapters the discussion of Native craftwork frames the subsequent interpretation of settler texts, the importance and sophistication of these discussions in fact far exceed that narrow frame. For example, though the second chapter focuses on settler-produced visual representations of Kateri Tekakwitha, Wigginton starts the chapter with an intricate account of Kanien:keha'ka aesthetics. The chapter identifies an artistic practice that blends hidden labor and overt skill, one that shapes those visual representations, of course, but that also compels a broader "practice of perception" that "seeks to apprehend, balance, and craft relationships between exterior surfaces and hidden interiors" (54). Here and elsewhere, chapters in *Indigenuity* that conclude ostensibly with claims about settler literatures in fact emphasize an interpretive approach that reorients and destabilizes settler-colonial expressions and epistemologies (201). Wigginton further reinforces this approach when she turns, at the close of each chapter, to the work of Indigenous artists in our current time (13). Thus, the third chapter, on the translation of "the sensation and craft of color" in eighteenth-century ethnologies of southeastern North America, concludes not with these accounts but rather with how Jeffrey Gibson and other Native artists from the region use a multisensorial perception of color to "create new stories and revivify connections to place" (86, 120). Each chapter ends in a similar manner, as Wigginton explains how "Indigenous creators continue to use and adapt" the knowledge found in craftwork to "survive and resist colonial displacement" (13).

Even absent these brief interpretive vignettes, this book would be an essential source in several fields. With them, *Indigenuity* seems a required text for an even larger cohort of scholars. Wigginton offers in *Indigenuity* an inventive and rigorous work of scholarship, one that—among its countless virtues—attests to how Indigenous studies will continue to invigorate and transform our understanding of the literary, bibliographical, and material histories of North America.

DANIEL RADUS is associate professor of English at SUNY Cortland.

SARA ČERNE

A Song over Miskwaa Rapids: A Novel
by Linda LeGarde Grover
University of Minnesota Press, 2023

WOMEN ELDERS, SEEN AND UNSEEN, hold together *A Song over Miskwaa Rapids*, a 2023 novel by Linda LeGarde Grover (Bois Forte Band of Ojibwe), as the opening dedication to "the mindimooyenyag" suggests. They predominate the list of friends and relatives that introduces characters in dramaturgical fashion; they shape the narrative from central stage and from behind the scenes; and they trigger the unraveling of history that takes place before the reader's eyes, influencing present events and revealing secrets that had remained buried for decades.

Although the novel shifts between 2022 and 1972, its cyclical timeline is not confined by the half century that these dates bookmark. Instead, *A Song over Miskwaa Rapids* shows how seemingly distant historical events play themselves out again and again in the lives of the people of Mozhay Point, a fictional reservation in northern Minnesota and the setting of LeGarde Grover's previous novels (*In the Night of Memory* [2020] and *The Road Back to Sweetgrass* [2016], both published by the University of Minnesota Press). Even without the context of the author's earlier work, the setting reveals a complex web of relationships, overlapping histories, and competing interests between individuals and different levels of government, ranging from federal to tribal, on the reservation and beyond, via Chicago and the Federal Relocation Program.

In many ways, land is at the center of the narrative, acting as a guardian of history, a catalyst for present events, and a character in its own right. "It was always about Sweetgrass," the piece of land at the center of the conflict, the narrator tells us, "for Zho Wash and the Muskrat family that became the Washingtons and lost the land, and for Margie and the LaForces who received the land as their allotment—and it still is" (134). *A Song over Miskwaa Rapids* sketches the different consequences and implications of an 1854 land cession treaty that established the borders of the Mozhay Point reservation, displacing families who did not sign the treaty and relocating those who did.

Invoking historical irony, the narrative centers on Margie Robineau and her efforts to keep Sweetgrass, the forty acres of land that were allotted to her ancestors the LaForces, from being purchased by the tribal government. In an effort to attract more non-Native visitors and aid economic development, the tribe needs Sweetgrass to build a road connecting the tribal center to the Miskwaa River State Park visitor center—built by the state of Minnesota and "run by the Mozhay Point Band members as a collaborative endeavor" (47)—overlooking the site to which "unallotted and unrecognized Indians" were displaced after being forced off Mozhay Point (18). Although a group of invisible ancestral women takes turns watching over Sweetgrass at night, in Margie's world, the land seems to be slipping further and further away. As the tribal chair points out before a ghost from the past starts to threaten the deal, the development will happen one way or another, and Margie will "end up getting her heart broken over a piece of land that will end belonging to the tribe, as it was before Mozhay was divided up into individual allotments" (51).

An intricate novel that explores the afterlives of many of the darker aspects of Indigenous history in Minnesota, *A Song over Miskwaa Rapids* also offers moments of humor and levity, many of which are provided by the unseen women elders as they comment on and intervene in current events. The prose is sharp, concise, and often unexpected, drawing on tradition while avoiding clichés, as it sets the stage and describes birdsong "passed down through more generations than birds or humans could count, over the land of Mozhay Point" (6). The novel's greatest strength is perhaps its embrace of nuance and ambiguity, which makes it a perfect companion to any classroom setting grappling with the complexities and contradictions that arose from the 1887 Dawes Act and its division of tribal lands into individual allotments.

Raising as many questions as it answers, *A Song over Miskwaa Rapids* provides a beautiful and utterly readable saga of this carefully mapped-out place, revealing the intersecting fates of several families and challenging preconceived notions of different characters' connections and motivations. Now privy to the ways the past lives on in the present at Mozhay Point, the reader is left with the interpretative work of piecing it all together and unearthing the full story.

SARA ČERNE is research grants program director at the University of California Humanities Research Institute.

JULIANNE NEWMARK

*My Heart Is Bound Up with Them: How Carlos Montezuma Became
the Voice of a Generation*
by David Martínez
University of Arizona Press, 2023

DAVID MARTÍNEZ'S *My Heart is Bound Up with Them* attends to the ways in which a familial, epistolary archive—The Carlos Montezuma collection at Arizona State University's Hayden Library—broadens our understanding of Dr. Carlos Montezuma's (Yavapai, 1866–1923) life and legacy. For scholars who are familiar with Montezuma through his work with the Society of American Indians (SAI) between 1911 and 1920, his *Wassaja* newsletter and his service as a medical doctor not only in Indian Bureau employ but also in private practice in Chicago, Martínez's sharp and focused new study will add crucial nuance to many scholars' long-held understandings. By focusing on letters written between a primary group of four people (Montezuma and Yavapai relations Charles Dickens, George Dickens, and Mike Burns) spanning the years 1901 to 1921, Martínez's compelling book conveys a new story about Montezuma and his tribal relations, his commitment to land and water rights in Arizona, and his evolving sense of his own roles relative to family, home, and place.

To many scholars in Indigenous studies, Montezuma is best known for his strident anti-Indian-Bureau stance, which marked his relationship with the SAI and was an unmistakable theme of *Wassaja*. As a subject of critical study, Montezuma was discussed in Hazel Hertzberg's impactful *The Search for an American Indian Identity: Modern Pan Indian Movements* (1971), among other important texts that focused specifically on him, including works by Peter Iverson and Leon Speroff. Regarding Herzberg's representations of Montezuma, Martínez rebukes her narrow view, which focused on his factionalism and "vehement disdain for the reservation system" (9). Yet, his crucial and lasting advocacy on the part of two Arizona communities— Fort McDowell (the community of his own ancestral people, the Yavapai) and Gila River (Martínez's community, the Akimel O'odham)—is a truth about Montezuma's life that Hertzberg (and others) either excluded or minimized. Martínez's work corrects neglectful and diminishing scholarly treatment of Montezuma and celebrates other scholars who have honored Montezuma's complexity, advocacy, and familial commitments. Martínez emphasizes this latter reality most, affording his volume its resonance. He writes: "Indigenous intellectuals are first and foremost someone's relative. They are members of their people's kinship relations who, because of their work and legacy, became revered ancestors" (164).

Martínez offers a compelling loop in this work; he connects Montezuma's advocacy work on behalf of his relatives at the Fort McDowell Mohave Apache Reservation to his work on "behalf of the O'odham," Martínez's people, "in which Montezuma most successfully and convincingly demonstrated his pan-Indian political beliefs. Yavapai and O'odham may be historic rivals, but they/we were united in the battle against Indian Bureau injustice" (17). Montezuma agitated against "the racist depravation of Indian water in Arizona," which "was a recurring problem not only for the Akimel O'odham but also the Yavapai" (25). Through such linkages, Martínez radically broadens readers' insights into Montezuma's life's work and his relationships to American bureaucracy, the reservation system, assimilationist pressures (such as those espoused by his mentor Richard Henry Pratt), and multilocal/cross-community relationality and kinship.

Across its seven central chapters (with titles including "The Unknown Indian Soldier: America Goes to War While Another Battle is Waged at Home" and "An Unexpected O'odham Hero: Montezuma's Legacy Beyond Fort McDowell"), *My Heart is Bound Up with Them* presents a nuanced view of Montezuma's significant impacts, as an advocate, relative, pan-Indian leader, three-time Agency physician, private-practice doctor, and writer. Many scholars are familiar with each compelling issue of Montezuma's *Wassaja,* but Martinez allows his readers' view to expand to the private correspondence (concerning interactions with local government agents, "Yavapai factionalism," rumors, intertribal dynamics, requests for Montezuma's intervention with Indian Bureau representatives and the commissioner, and more) that was ongoing throughout this period. Martinez also catalogues historical and critical attention to Montezuma over the years, providing comprehensive coverage of how Montezuma has been taken up in the literature. This is valuable historiographical work, emphasizing the variations across the last century of interest in different aspects of Montezuma's biography. Above all, Martínez allows what might be perceived as an academic, historical study to transcend genre parameters, following the model of Montezuma himself, wherein professional and personal passions were interwoven and were, thereby, strengthened. While Martínez's study has Montezuma as its *prima facie* focus, Martínez presents Montezuma's voice as "one of a community of voices, in which each voice has a story to tell about enduring, surviving, resisting, and overcoming the occupation and exploitation of their ancestral homes" (166).

Martínez's volume insists upon such coexistence, thereby forging new scholarly understandings of Montezuma and his legacy.

JULIANNE NEWMARK is director of technical and professional communication and assistant chair for core writing at the University of New Mexico.

DEONDRE SMILES

City of Dispossessions: Indigenous Peoples, African Americans,
  and the Creation of Modern Detroit
by Kyle T. Mays
University of Pennsylvania Press, 2022

THE CITY OF DETROIT has become synonymous in public consciousness with both the automobile industry as well as urban topics such as decline, decay, and more recently, resurgence. Beneath the surface of modern Detroit exists a long legacy of shifting geographies and connections to land and space, particularly among its Black and Indigenous inhabitants. This is the history that Kyle Mays takes up in *City of Dispossession,* with a focus on the ways in which that history has been erased and whitewashed in the creation of modern-day Detroit. Starting from the dispossession of the land that comprises what is claimed as Detroit by European settlers, to the dispossession of Indigenous identity, to the continued subjugation of Indigenous (and Black) spaces in Detroit at the hands of industry and neoliberalization, Mays works to remind the reader that even the most mundane spaces can conceal the deep violences that helped enable settler claims to them.

While Mays does provide a historical narrative of the ways in which dispossession functioned in Detroit in both historical and contemporary contexts, he makes it clear that his focus is not on simply retelling the histories of Detroit but focusing on the various forms of dispossession that helped to make the city what it is. Mays speaks to the inherent anxieties that white settlers possessed toward the "others" they shared the city with—first, they stole Indigenous lands to secure their political and economic futures, then they focused on co-opting Indigenous identity in a way that further overwrote and dispossessed Indigenous connections to the land in favor of a modern framing of white Detroit. This was followed with the exploitation of Black labor in the city, followed by the further marginalization of Black and Indigenous communities as white Detroitians fled to the suburbs and devalued the city and its institutions.

Of course, a purely trauma-based perspective obscures the ways in which people endure. Mays also writes of the resurgence and resilience of Black and Indigenous communities in Detroit in asserting and maintaining their identities and connections to space and place. Rather than being totally relegated to a forgotten past, Mays writes on the ways in which understanding and highlighting Indigenous histories in Detroit also can lead to greater visibility for Black histories and geographies. The various intersecting geographies that comprise the city today are illuminated by Mays' writings. I am strongly reminded of Tiffany Lethabo King's *The Black Shoals* when reading Mays' accounts of the shifting and complex geographical identities of Detroit as well as the people within it. Mays' work teases apart the prevailing idea that settler colonial geographers involve a settler/Indigenous dyad by describing the ways in which Detroit is also part of Black geographical understandings. He also extends the analysis further by contemplating ideas of Black Indigeneity, a topic that has picked up currency in discussions around Indigenous identity and belonging in the United States and Canada today. Similar to King, Mays dives into the "messiness" of such politics—he speaks, for example, of the ways in which Indigenous Peoples have achieved moments of visibility in the eyes of white settlers, although this has come at the expense of *de facto* allying themselves with racist settler structures.

This provides a very valuable point of inquiry, as it tends to the ways in which relationships between Indigenous Peoples, Black peoples, and their respective geographies play out in urban contexts. While there is plenty of scholarship on urban Indigenous politics and urban Black politics, this book provides one of the first accounts where these aspects are brought together. This is of deep interest to me from both an academic and personal standpoint, being a Black Native who grew up in urban spaces.

I found myself recommending this book to several different groups of people in my professional and personal orbit—many of my friends come from Detroit and have been unaware of the Indigenous histories of the city, and so I recommended it to them—but I also recommend it to people who are interested in the intersections of Blackness and Indigeneity within settler colonial geographies and the ways in which they overcome and exceed the spatial constraints placed upon them not only historically but also in the present day.

NIIYOKAMIGAABAW DEONDRE SMILES is assistant professor of geography at the University of Victoria, British Columbia, Canada.

TIM FRANDY

From Lapland to Sápmi: Collecting and Returning Sámi Craft and Culture
by Barbara Sjoholm
University of Minnesota Press, 2023

OVER THE PAST DECADE, Swedish-American author Barbara Sjoholm has established herself as a prolific translator and author of books involving Sámi culture and the Danish ethnographer Emelie Demant-Hatt, whose collaborations with Johan Turi produced the first published secular book in a Sámi language in 1910, *Muitalus Sámiid Birra.* Sjoholm's earlier translations of Demant-Hatt's *By the Fire* (2019) and *With the Lapps in the High Mountains* (2013), in particular, have brought important Sámi primary source materials from Danish to English, and contributed meaningfully to the recirculation of older ethnographic materials to contemporary Sámi and Sámi diasporic audiences.

In her latest book, *From Lapland to Sápmi,* Sjoholm chronicles the collection and exhibition of Sámi material culture and intangible cultural heritage: their sometimes-forcible extraction; their storage and display in museums throughout the Nordic countries and Europe; and the slow process of repatriation and rematriation of these materials. The work's primary focus—likely because of the complexities of working across vastly different languages—is on Norway and Sweden, though Finnish- and Russian-side Sámi also figure into the work to some extent.

Always a gifted writer, Sjoholm weaves together compelling stories of the people involved with these processes of extraction, exhibition, and return. These extractions and exhibitions have involved some of the most painful episodes in Sámi history—including the confiscation and destruction of sacred *noaidi* drums, the compulsory nude photography collected for use by racial biologists, the theft and trade of Sámi human remains, and the exhibition of Sámi people in human zoos. Further, the stories of these cultural items' return are recognized as among the most powerful moments in recent Sámi history: the emergence of Sámi museums as cultural infrastructure, the return and reburial of human remains, and the repatriation of Sámi drums and other historical artifacts. In this regard, Sjoholm's work documents in detail an important and still-emerging story of restoring cultural sovereignty that will continue to be significant in Sápmi for generations to come.

Sjoholm's focus in the book is largely on historical collection and exhibition outside of Sápmi, with only about 20 percent of the work focused on repatriation. The unfortunate consequence is that much of the work is focused extensively on non-Sámi ethnographers, who overshadow even many of the well-known Sámi who are occasionally introduced in the text. Some of these choices are, of course, mandated by limited historical documentation that seldom gives individual agency to Sámi artists, singers, storytellers, and cultural leaders. Nonetheless, the net effect serves as a painful reminder that while Sámi were shamed and persecuted for keeping their culture and language alive, many celebrated non-Sámi academics, museologists, and collectors traded in the wares of a supposedly "dying" culture for status, prestige, and fun.

The book is at its best where Sjoholm lends agency to Sámi individuals: for instance, her detailed account of Lars Jakobsen Hætta's life in prison and his collaborations with Jens Andreas Friis; or her summary of Outi Pieski and Eeva-Kristiina Harlin's work to revitalize the *ládjogahpir* woman's hat, which was formerly termed the "devil's horn" and burned by missionaries as they worked to subvert women's agency in Sámi communities.

Sjoholm's work straddles a difficult line between academic and journalistic writing. Although the book is well-researched, scholars may be frustrated by the lack of a citation trail to primary source materials in order to form their own critical opinions and interpretations of events. Although there is a sizable selected bibliography, and citations are included throughout the work, it remains unclear for much of the text where extremely detailed biographical portraits or articulated interpretations of historical events emerge from: whether from preexisting publications, personal journals, oral accounts, photographs, or the author's own interpretation. Similarly, from a scholarly perspective, additional engagement with the scholarship of museum studies, ethnology, Indigenous studies, and religious studies could have further benefited this well-conceived project's theoretical orientation. Sjoholm's approach is accessible to a general audience but does not fully enter the conversations that have existed in these fields for decades.

Overall, however, Sjoholm's work is of value for educators, a general audience, and—despite the problematic citation issues—for researchers wishing to further engage with historical ethnographies and collections across multiple languages. It tells detailed stories of the extraction, trade, and display of Sámi culture by non-Sámi and of the deep impact that the return of Sámi craft and intangible cultural heritage has had on recent generations of Sámi people.

TIM FRANDY (Sámi American) is assistant professor in the Department of Central, Eastern, and Northern European Studies, University of British Columbia, Vancouver, Canada.

KATRINA M. PHILLIPS

Voicing Identity: Cultural Appropriation and Indigenous Issues
edited by John Borrows and Kent McNeil
University of Toronto Press, 2022

THE QUESTION OF CULTURAL APPROPRIATION has long haunted nearly every aspect of Native and Indigenous studies. From popular culture and academia to fashion and the law, debates over what constitutes appropriation and what could be considered appreciation continue nearly unabated. Within academia, the questions often seem even more pronounced: how—and who—can research, write, and teach about Indigenous people? In *Voicing Identity*, John Borrows and Kent McNeil have assembled fifteen essays that aim to demonstrate how to teach and research respectfully, and how to do so in a way that promotes a greater understanding of Indigenous cultures and histories. The essays within the volume are often profoundly personal, drawing on the lived experiences of both the Indigenous and non-Indigenous contributors. Borrows and McNeil contend that, despite the variety of backgrounds and beliefs, these authors have come together through their "common commitment to dismantle the legacy of colonialism" (11).

The legacy of colonialism—mostly in Canada, but occasionally in the United States—lurks in the background of nearly every essay. For Sarah Morales, it is the researcher's responsibility to locate oneself in relation to their work, while Emma Feltes details how her work on the 1980s Constitution Express was and still is guided by the principles of the Indigenous Peoples she works with. In the same vein, kQwa'st'not Charlene George and Hannah Askew's coauthored chapter asks the reader to consider four questions about relationality and relationship-building. Aimée Craft considers the ethics of appropriation (or misappropriation) and being a good relative. Lindsay Borrows highlights both the consequences of lateral violence and the importance of learning (and learning from) the Anishinaabe language and Anishinaabe teachings.

For other authors, their own family histories bear witness to how they approach their work. For Sa'ke'j Henderson, his upbringing in Oklahoma and subsequent participation in the movement to remove Native mascots marks a key point in his life. Keith Thor Carlson turns to what he considers the "conundrum of double permanence," or the fact that Canada's economic and political systems are not designed to support both Indigenous people and settler Canadians (34). For Hadley Friedland, her childhood shapes her engagement with the spiritual, sacred, or ceremonial aspects of Indigenous legal traditions. Other non-Indigenous scholars like Robert Hamilton outline numerous factors that non-Indigenous people who see themselves as allies should consider when approaching Indigenous histories and contemporary issues. Michael Asch uses four lived experiences to show how he conducts himself as a non-Indigenous scholar engaging with Indigenous issues, demonstrating, for Asch, the complexity inherent in academic research.

Questions of law and legality also run through the volume. Karen Drake and A. Christian Airhart turn to the question of who should teach Indigenous law, particularly in the wake of the 2015 Truth and Reconciliation Commission. Hamar Foster examines the 2017 decision of the Benchers of the Law Society to remove a statue of Sir Matthew Baillie Begbie, who presided over the 1864 trials of six Tsilhqot'in warriors and earned the nickname "the Hanging Judge." Felix Hoehn's essay centers the Crown's historic and continuing denial of Indigenous sovereignty, arguing for "a just foundation for a positive relationship between Indigenous Peoples in Canada and non-Indigenous Canadians" (110). Joshua Nichols interrogates the consequences of the use of "Aboriginal peoples" and the subsequent contestations over the phrase "Aboriginal perspective" in regard to the *Constitution Act, 1982.* For John Borrows, claims of cultural appropriation "hide as much as they reveal" (157). The "Indigenous legal context of our engagements," as Borrows argues, should guide our approaches to these conversations. Canada's "deeply colonial constitution" aims to "maintain the fiction that all governing powers derive from the Crown" (162).

Taken on their own, the chapters read almost as soliloquies (and occasionally duets). When taken together, though, the essays become a thundering chorus against colonialism and cultural appropriation, speaking to the power inherent in Native and Indigenous histories—power that has carried through to the present. I applaud the editors for compiling an array of stories that touch on such broad themes and topics, and I thank them for trusting their contributing authors and finding ways to connect these far-reaching and wide-ranging issues. All the essays are written in the first person, which simply goes to show how deeply embedded and closely tied these questions of appropriation and Indigenous issues continue to be. This work is far from finished, but the essays in this volume underscore the importance and necessity of these ongoing conversations.

KATRINA M. PHILLIPS (Red Cliff Ojibwe) is associate professor of history at Macalester College.

JOSEPH BAUERKEMPER

American Indian Tribal Governance: A Critical Perspective
by Stephen Wall
Tribal College Press, 2023

STEPHEN WALL OFFERS what many *NAIS* readers will view as a familiar explanation for why he set about crafting his book, *American Indian Tribal Governance.* The project arose due to the lack of available teaching materials. In Wall's case, he set about putting together tribal governance courses at the Institute of American Indian Arts. Learning opportunities focused on tribal government are happily of increasing interest to graduate and undergraduate students. When such courses need to serve students from a variety of backgrounds, experiences, and homelands, however—there remains a lack of readily applicable teaching texts. With this book, Wall has succeeded in addressing this scarcity, while also making noteworthy scholarly and applied contributions. He has created instructional material that he and many others require, and he has enhanced scholarly and applied discourses regarding Indigenous governance in U.S. contexts.

Ultimately oriented toward "the development of tribal institutions and tribal capacity," (4) the book first presents a theoretical overview of concepts fundamental to tribal governance and then moves into a sustained consideration of tribal governance institutions. Wall appropriately and necessarily locates the entire project in relation to Indigenous sovereignty and cultures, while unavoidably illuminating U.S. federal Indian policy and trust doctrine as deeply influential—yet never decisive—elements of the colonial context. He also emphasizes the separation of powers as it variously is and is not applied in tribal governance. Chapters on tribal constitutions, policymaking bodies, the work of tribal administration, judicial systems, and intergovernmental diplomacy round out the volume. Finally, a substantial epilogue surveys the challenges, opportunities, and exceptionally high stakes of contemporary tribal governance, culminating in a committed and even radical appeal to innovative traditions of self-determined governance and political economy.

The book's twelve chapters are concise and imminently accessible, inviting academic, student, and practitioner readers. Each of these audiences is well-served by the text, which contributes to the growing scholarly field of tribal administration and governance, offers undergraduate and graduate instructors a wide-ranging pedagogical tool, and encourages current and future leaders and civil servants to prioritize self-governance grounded in land and in cultural traditions and knowledge.

A broad and diverse array of *NAIS* readers can and should make good use of Wall's book. I am particularly eager to put, initially, excerpted chapters in the hands of students pursuing applied education in tribal governance. Producing relevant teaching material was a primary motivation for Wall, and I expect that many students and their instructors will benefit from the book so deployed. This should, moreover, have longer-term and meaningful impact as those students move further into their careers shaping the work of Indigenous governments.

Scholars, writers, and researchers across many subfields of Indigenous studies will find the book to be a useful reference for connecting any manner of work to the fundamentals of Indigenous governance. Simply put, it offers a thorough survey and capable primer for those new to thinking deeply about tribal governance. At the same time, the book also productively engages the well-seasoned reader. Whether working within or well beyond the U.S., scholars should appreciate that the book suitably represents the current state of U.S.-based scholarship on Indigenous governance, a terrain both increasingly critical in its orientation and readily liable to critique. Wall neither pursues a comparative framework in the book nor situates it in relation to global Indigenous studies. This is a matter of scope rather than oversight. There is, after all, already plenty of complexity for Wall to grapple with here.

JOSEPH BAUERKEMPER is professor of American Indian studies and director of the Tribal Sovereignty Institute at the University of Minnesota Duluth.

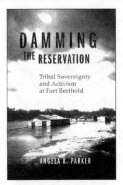
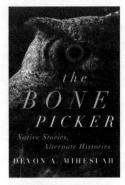
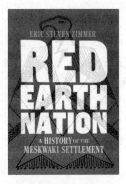
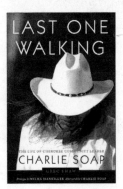
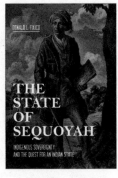

Yale UNIVERSITY PRESS

Empty Spaces
Jordan Abel

**Violent
Appetites**
*Hunger in the
Early Northeast*
Carla Cevasco

Talking Back
*Native Women
and the Making of
the Early South*
Alejandra
Dubcovsky

**Catching
the Light**
Joy Harjo
Why I Write

**Providence and
the Invention
of American
History**
Sarah Koenig

Squanto
A Native Odyssey
Andrew Lipman

**California, a
Slave State**
Jean Pfaelzer
The Lamar Series in
Western History

**Jaune Quick-to-
See Smith**
Memory Map
Laura Phipps
Distributed for Whitney
Museum of American Art

THE HENRY ROE CLOUD SERIES ON
AMERICAN INDIANS AND MODERNITY

**The Rediscovery
of America**
*Native Peoples
and the Unmaking
of U.S. History*
Ned Blackhawk

**Indigenous
Visions**
*Rediscovering
the World of
Franz Boas*
Edited by
Ned Blackhawk
and Isaiah
Lorado Wilner

Memory Lands
*King Philip's War
and the Place of
Violence in the
Northeast*
Christine M.
DeLucia

**"Vaudeville
Indians" on
Global Circuits,
1880s to 1930s**
Christine Bold

**The Makings
and Unmakings
of Americans**
*Indians and
Immigrants
in American
Literature
and Culture,
1879-1924*
Cristina Stanciu

**Assembled
for Use**
*Indigenous
Compilation
and the Archives
of Early Native
American
Literatures*
Kelly Wisecup

AVAILABLE IN PAPERBACK

Playing Indian
Philip J. Deloria
With a New
Preface
Yale Historical
Publications Series

California
*An American
History*
John Mack
Faragher

In Our Hands
*Native
Photography,
1890 to Now*
Edited by Jill
Ahlberg Yohe,
Jaida Grey Eagle,
and Casey Riley
Distributed for the
Minneapolis Institute
of Art

yalebooks.com

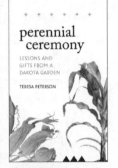
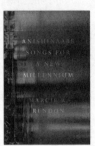